Filling Up America:
An Economic-Demographic Model of Population Growth and Distribution in the Nineteenth-Century United States

INDUSTRIAL DEVELOPMENT AND THE SOCIAL FABRIC, VOLUME 8
Editor: John P. McKay, *Department of History, University of Illinois*

INDUSTRIAL DEVELOPMENT AND THE SOCIAL FABRIC

An International Series of Historical Monographs

Edited by **John P. McKay**
Department of History
University of Illinois

Volume 1. **Forums of Order: The Federal Courts and Business in American History**
Tony Allan Freyer, *University of Arkansas, Little Rock*

Volume 2. **Competition and Regulation: The Development of Oligopoly in the Meat Packing Industry**
Mary Yeager, *University of California, Los Angeles*

Volume 3. **Keeping the Corporate Image: Public Relations and Business, 1900-1950**
Richard S. Tedlow, *Graduate School of Business Administration, Harvard University*

Volume 4. **The Growth of a Refining Region**
Joseph A. Pratt, *School of Business Administration, University of California, Berkeley*

Volume 5. **Business and Government in the Oil Industry: A Case Study of Sun Oil, 1876-1945**
August W. Giebelhaus, *Georgia Institute of Technology*

Volume 6. **Pioneering a Modern Small Business: Wakefield Seafoods and the Alaskan Frontier**
Mansel G. Blackford, *Ohio State University*

Volume 7. **The End of the Practical Man: Higher Education and the Institutionalization of Entrepreneurial Performance in Germany, France, and Great Britain — 1880 to 1940**
Robert R. Locke, *European Institute for Advanced Study in Management*

Volume 8. **Filling Up America: An Economic-Demographic Model of Population Growth and Distribution in the Nineteenth-Century United States**
Morton Owen Schapiro, *Williams College*

To My Family,
Jeanette, Howard, Judy and Mimi

Filling Up America:
An Economic-Demographic Model of Population Growth and Distribution in the Nineteenth-Century United States

by MORTON OWEN SCHAPIRO
Department of Economics
Williams College

JAI PRESS INC.

Greenwich, Connecticut *London, England*

Library of Congress Cataloging-in-Publication Data

Schapiro, Morton Owen.
Filling up America.

(Industrial development and the social fabric ; v. 8)
Bibliography: p.
Includes index.
1. United States—Population—History—19th century.
2. United States—Population, Rural—History—
19th century. 3. Fertility, Human—United States—
History—19th century. 4. Migration, Internal—
United States—History—19th century. 5. United States—
Economic conditions—To 1865. 6. United States—
Economic conditions—1865–1918. I. Title. II. Series.
HB3505.S33 1986 304.6′0973 86-2771
ISBN 0-89232-675-1

36 Sherwood Place
Greenwich, Connecticut 06830

JAI PRESS LTD.
3 Henrietta Street
London WC2E 8LU
England

ISBN: 0-89232-675-1

Library of Congress Catalog Card Number: 86-2771

Manufactured in the United States of America

CONTENTS

List of Tables

Preface

The recent increase in interest in the study of economic demography has resulted in a growing number of studies dealing with contemporary population issues in the developed and developing world. The historical counterpart has been largely limited to the study of Europe, with the United States being relatively neglected. Further, those studies which apply economic models to U.S. population history have concentrated on partial equilibrium analyses which assume that all other factors affecting population change other than the one in question are determined outside their models. This severely constrains the ability of these studies to quantitatively evaluate many of the long-standing hypotheses put forth by economists, demographers and historians concerning the causes and consequences of population growth and distribution in the historical United States.

One of these hypotheses is Frederick Jackson Turner's notion that the frontier acted as a safety valve by dissipating the pressures of overpopulation which had led to social upheaval in other nations throughout the world. Another is Thomas Malthus' proposition that the ultimate check on population growth is an increase in mortality with fertility being almost completely unresponsive to changes in the economic environment. A third hypothesis was proposed by Francis Walker, the first president of the American Economic Association, who speculated that U.S. immigration led to a decline in native fertility as economic competition increased. A more general set of concerns relates to the role of land availability in explaining the observed fertility decline—a decline which, in light of stable mortality, represents a strong refutation of demographic transition theory.

This book attempts to fill some of the void. By using partial equilibrium analysis, fertility and migration are examined separately in an attempt to evaluate the impact of changes in economic factors—in particular, changes in the availability of farmland—in explaining cross-section and time-series movements in birth rates and in gross migration. More importantly, the fertility and migration models are combined and, after a number of additions, a general dynamic model is produced. The structure of this model allows for an analysis of the settlement of the United States in which population growth and distribution affect the economic environment and initiate a demographic response which, in turn, dictates the course of further population growth. The model is used to evaluate empirically the hypotheses described above and to provide insight into those factors which played important roles in determining the course of U.S. demographic history.

My interest in this subject evolved during graduate training at the University of Pennsylvania. Richard A. Easterlin's courses in economic history and economic demography marked the beginning of my work in these fields and two and a half years spent as his research assistant gave me the opportunity to delve more deeply into these areas. My dissertation, "An Economic Model of Fertility, Migration, and Settlement in the Rural Northern United States: 1790–1900," under his supervision, represented a first attempt to model the U.S. settlement process and further research has led to substantial revisions and extensions, culminating in the present volume.

There are many people I would like to thank for their advice and encouragement. My dissertation committee of Richard A. Easterlin, chairman, Jere R. Behrman, Samuel H. Preston, and Anne D. Williams offered many helpful comments on my earlier work as did Dennis A. Ahlburg, George Alter, Robert D. Cohen, Gretchen A. Condran, Eileen M. Crimmins, Mahmoud S. Issa, Shireen J. Jejeebhoy, and Frank R. Lichtenberg. Subsequent research was greatly facilitated by the suggestions of Roger E. Bolton, Michael S. McPherson and other participants in the Williams College Economics Seminar.

The bulk of this manuscript was written while I was an Adsit

Fellow on leave from Williams College in residence as a Visiting Assistant Professor of Economics at the University of Southern California. I would like to thank the President and Trustees of Williams College for their financial support and Dennis J. Aigner, chairman of the U.S.C. economics department, for allowing me complete use of the support facilities during my stay. Special thanks to Sharon Koga for typing several versions of this manuscript with extraordinary efficiency.

I would like to single out a few people to whom I am particularly indebted. Eric F. Smith did a superb job of programming and also provided a number of insightful comments. Two of my Williams colleagues, Lee J. Alston and Gordon C. Winston, repeatedly offered valuable suggestions and encouragement which were essential to the completion of the book. Richard A. Easterlin, as a mentor, employer, colleague and friend, has been and continues to be an important source of inspiration. Finally, my deepest gratitude goes to my parents, Jeanette Klafter Schapiro and Dr. Howard F. Schapiro, my sister, Judy Schapiro, and my wife, Mimi Rothman Schapiro, to whom this book is respectfully dedicated.

Chapter I

Introduction

I.1 THE SCOPE OF THE ANALYSIS

The principal goal of this study is to identify those factors which contributed to the settlement of a large and important section of the United States: the rural north.[1] The pattern of rural population growth in 23 states within this region is examined during the period in which the greatest part of the settlement process occurred, 1790 to 1900.[2]

An examination of the buildup of population within rural areas of the northern states shows a relatively uniform pattern of population growth across states. Initially, states experienced very low rates of population increase but, eventually, a sustained period of rapid population growth took place. Finally, the growth of the rural population slowed and a stable population was reached.[3] While this basic pattern was reproduced in each of the states under consideration, it differed to some extent depending on the period of time in which the growth of the rural population had taken place. States which were settled toward the latter part of the nineteenth century were characterized by a more rapid rise in rural population and, therefore, the pattern of rural population growth was condensed relative to those states which had been settled at earlier dates. Further, the experience of the individual states was mirrored by the area as a whole as the buildup of the total rural population for the northern region started slowly, accelerated, and then leveled off.

The pattern outlined above is shown in Tables I.1 and I.2. The measure of the level of settlement for the entire area and for each state is a density variable. At each date, the actual rural population is divided by the rural population in the year when the buildup of the population had ceased.[4] Thus, this variable represents the percentage of the maximum rural population reached at a given date (or, the percentage of the settlement process completed) and the degree of rural settlement is measured by summing across states (Table I.1) or by examining individual states (Table I.2).

While the pattern of rural settlement within the northern United States is clear, the reasons underlying this pattern are not. What determined the date of initial settlement for each state? Why did the rate of population growth in rural areas of each state increase after a relatively slow population buildup and then decrease as some maximum population level was approached? Why did states which were settled relatively late experience more rapid population growth than those settled earlier? What was the role of immigration in the settlement of the rural north? These questions are addressed after an examination of the determinants of population growth.

Table I.1. Ratio of Rural Population in 23 Northern States to Maximum Rural Population, 1790 to 1900

1900	.938
1890	.890
1880	.819
1870	.692
1860	.593
1850	.458
1840	.358
1830	.264
1820	.201
1810	.149
1800	.110
1790	.085

Source: Calculated from Table 20, Vol. I, Part 1, U.S. Census, 1960.

Table I.2. Ratio of Rural Population of Each of the 23 Northern States to Maximum Rural Population, 1790 to 1900

State	*1790*	*1800*	*1810*	*1820*	*1830*	*1840*	*1850*	*1860*	*1870*	*1880*	*1890*	*1900*
Maine	.18	.28	.42	.55	.74	.88	.96	1.00	—	—	—	—
New Hampshire	.52	.68	.79	.90	.97	.97	1.00	—	—	—	—	—
Vermont	.28	.50	.71	.76	.91	.95	1.00	—	—	—	—	—
Massachusetts	.66	.72	.75	.81	.85	.92	.99	1.00	—	—	—	—
Rhode Island	.83	.82	.88	.96	1.00	—	—	—	—	—	—	—
Connecticut	.63	.65	.67	.69	.74	.74	.85	.92	.98	.99	1.00	—
New York	.13	.22	.36	.51	.69	.83	.94	1.00	—	—	—	—
New Jersey	.33	.38	.43	.49	.55	.60	.73	.82	.92	.93	.97	1.00
Pennsylvania	.14	.19	.25	.32	.40	.50	.62	.70	.77	.88	.95	1.00
Delaware	.56	.61	.69	.69	.73	.66	.74	.86	.89	.93	.93	.94
Maryland	.48	.49	.52	.54	.56	.56	.62	.71	.76	.88	.86	.94
Ohio	.00	.02	.11	.26	.42	.66	.80	.89	.91	1.00	—	—
Indiana	.00	.00	.01	.09	.21	.41	.57	.75	.87	.96	.97	1.00
Illinois	—	.00	.01	.03	.07	.21	.36	.67	.88	.97	.96	1.00
Michigan	—	.00	.00	.01	.02	.14	.25	.44	.64	.83	.92	.99
Wisconsin	—	—	—	—	.00	.02	.20	.48	.61	.72	.82	.92
Minnesota	—	—	—	—	—	.00	.00	.12	.28	.47	.65	.86
Iowa	—	—	—	—	.00	.03	.11	.37	.63	.83	.91	1.00
Missouri	—	—	.01	.03	.07	.19	.30	.50	.65	.82	.92	1.00
North Dakota	—	—	—	—	—	—	—	—	.00	.06	.32	.52
South Dakota	—	—	—	—	—	—	—	.00	.02	.16	.57	.64
Nebraska	—	—	—	—	—	—	.00	.03	.11	.44	.86	.91
Kansas	—	—	—	—	—	—	.00	.08	.27	.77	1.00	—

Source: Calculated from Table 20, Vol. I, Part 1, U.S. Census, 1960.

Population growth is a function of the three basic components of demographic change: fertility, migration, and mortality. While each of these elements are discussed in the chapters that follow, the first two components are of primary interest. Historical fertility and migration data are fragmentary but, nonetheless, the overall movement in these factors over time is discernable. Within states, rural fertility rates declined over time while the migration balance eventually shifted from net in-migration to net out-migration. For the entire region, rural fertility rates decreased precipitously throughout the period under examination while the amount of east-west and rural-urban migration increased. An understanding of the relationship between the settlement pattern described above and the decline in rural fertility, the change to net out-migration, and the increase in urban and westward migration is the key to explaining that pattern. Was the decline in rural fertility and the increase in east-west and rural-urban migration a response to the increase in population density which occurred as a state achieved more advanced levels of settlement? In turn, to what extent did changes in fertility and migration affect the further buildup of the population? These questions address a central issue of this study: did population growth have economic ramifications which caused the observed movements in fertility and migration, and did these latter movements bring the growth of the rural population to a halt? If so, what does this imply about Malthus' famous hypothesis that an increase in mortality is the eventual check on population growth?

The approach used here in answering these questions is as follows. First, specification and estimation of fertility and migration models within a partial equilibrium context is undertaken in order to suggest whether or not movements in demographic variables were the result of changes in the economic environment which accompanied population growth. Next, the fertility and migration models are combined to form a settlement model which attempts to replicate the course of population growth and distribution within rural areas of the northern states during the period 1790 to 1900. By adopting a general dynamic approach in which the relationship between fertility, migration and population growth are examined within a single model, the impacts of changes in fertility and migration in terms of rural settlement are explored. In addition, by altering various equations within the model, the relative importance of the different demographic variables (immigration, rural-urban migration and fertility) in accounting for the buildup of the rural population is seen and Frederick Jackson Turner's notion of a safety valve preventing excessive population pressure in the northern states is examined. In this way, the causes and the consequences of changes in the demographic determinants of population growth are analyzed and the settlement of the rural northern United States is explained. Lastly, the U.S. population experience is compared with the situation in today's developing countries with the intent of determining what lessons, if any, can be learned from U.S. demographic and economic history.

I.2 ORGANIZATION OF THE BOOK

Chapters II and III contain the fertility analysis. A theoretical model of fertility determination is outlined in Chapter II and applied to the demographic transition and to the specific case of the historical United States. An empirical model is specified and estimated in Chapter III and crude birth rate and rate of natural increase estimates are produced for each state, beginning with the decade 1790–1800 and concluding with the decade 1890–1900.

The theory of internal migration is discussed in Chapter IV and, in Chapter V, a gravity-type model is specified and estimated using data from the 1850 Census. The fertility and migration models are then combined to form a settlement model which is presented in Chapter VI. A control solution is produced by the original settlement model and its estimates are contrasted with the results from three alternative scenarios: no European immigration, no rural to urban migration, and no rural fertility decline. In this way, the role that each of these seemingly important factors played in determining the course of U.S. population growth and distribution is quantitatively evaluated.

Finally, in Chapter VII, conclusions from the U.S. analysis are outlined and population problems in the developing world are examined in terms of the historical experience of the United States.

NOTES

1. The U.S. was overwhelmingly rural during most of the period under examination with over ninety percent of the northern population residing in rural areas in 1810, over eighty-five percent in 1840, and still over seventy percent as late as 1870. While this analysis deals with population growth in rural areas, the role of urbanization is studied in detail in Chapter VI when the impact of rural-urban migration on rural population growth is explored.
2. These states are Maine, New Hampshire, Vermont, Massachusetts, Rhode Island, Connecticut, New York, New Jersey, Pennsylvania, Delaware, Maryland, Ohio, Indiana, Illinois, Michigan, Wisconsin, Minnesota, Iowa, Missouri, North Dakota, South Dakota, Nebraska and Kansas. See Chapter III for a discussion of why these states were chosen.
3. Renewed rural population growth took place in most states during the twentieth century but this is outside of the scope of this study.
4. Chapter III contains a more detailed discussion of settlement level and land availability proxies.

Chapter II

The Theory of Fertility

During the nineteenth century the United States underwent a large-scale reduction in fertility levels.[1] This decline was not limited to a particular segment of the population but, rather, affected the population as a whole.[2] The experience of the United States is particularly interesting in light of the fact that fertility rates began to fall by 1800 at the latest, while it appears that mortality rates were stable until the late nineteenth century.[3] This violates one conception of the demographic transition, which states that the decline in fertility is a lagged response to the reduction in mortality. Moreover, it is even in violation of a weaker version of the demographic transition, which allows for the concurrent decline in fertility and mortality rates. Thus the experience of the United States is highly unusual and is especially enigmatic since there is little evidence of a widespread decline in fertility preceding the decline in mortality in the demographic history of most other countries.[4] This chapter sets out a theoretical model of fertility determination (II.1) which is then applied to the historical United States (II.2). Conclusions are presented in the final section (II.3).

II.1 A GENERAL THEORETICAL MODEL OF FERTILITY DETERMINATION

In order to review systematically alternative hypotheses that attempt to explain the decline in U.S. fertility during the nineteenth century, a theoretical framework along the lines of Easterlin is employed.[5] This framework examines the relationship between fertility levels and three causal factors: the demand for children, C^d, the natural supply of children, C^n, and the costs of fertility regulation, CFR.

Figure II.1 shows that at some early stage of development (Stage I), it is likely that there existed an excess demand for surviving children.[6] The natural supply of surviving children (the number of surviving children in the absence of a conscious effort to restrict fertility) is limited by high mortality rates, low fecundity, and the existence of social practices (such as lactation) that increase the average birth interval. The demand for children is high because of a low price of children (relative to market goods) resulting from low direct (housing, food, and so on) and indirect (opportunity) costs net of the child's contribution to family income, high tastes for children (because of social norms concerning extended families) and low material aspirations (the amount of market goods desired before children are demanded is small due to limited exposure to these goods). At this stage, $C^d > C^n$, and there is no incentive to restrict fertility. Hence, the fertility rate, C, is equal to the natural rate.

Eventually, a second stage is reached as development leads to a decline in the demand for children (as tastes for children decline, the relative price of children increases and material aspirations are raised) and an increase in the natural supply (as fecundity increases, lactation becomes less prevalent, and mor-

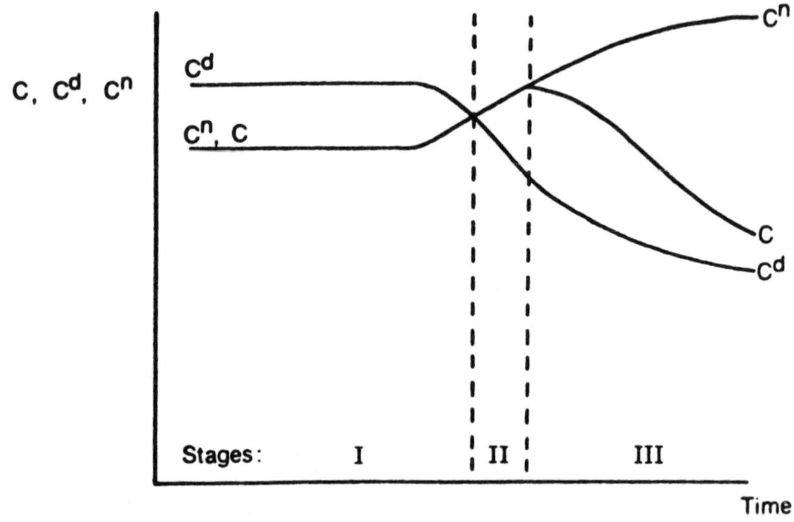

Figure II.1. The Stages of Fertility Determination.

tality rates decrease). Then, $C^n > C^d$ and there is an excess supply of children but, as in Stage I, no conscious effort to restrict fertility is attempted and $C = C^n$. Fertility regulation is attempted only when the disutility associated with limiting fertility (the monetary and psychic costs) is outweighed by the disutility associated with unregulated fertility. In Stage III, the costs of fertility regulation have declined (as information is disseminated and social mores change) while the costs of unregulated fertility have increased (as the natural fertility rate increases and the demand decreases), and fertility regulation practices begin. As long as the disutility associated with fertility regulation remains positive, it is unlikely that the actual number of surviving children would equal the desired number. Thus, $C^n > C > C^d$ with C approaching C^d as development levels increase.

The demographic transition, the change from high fertility and mortality to low fertility and mortality, takes place between Stages I and III. At Stage I, high mortality and a large C^d lead to a situation where the number of surviving children is equal to the natural rate which, while less than the desired number, is nonetheless at relatively high levels. In Stage II, the decline in mortality leads to an increase in natural fertility and the eventual transition to stage III where mortality continues to decline and fertility regulation commences. Hence, the traditional conception of the demographic transition in which a mortality decline precedes the fertility decline is consistent with the general fertility model described above. The modified demographic transition theory in which the mortality and fertility declines occur simultaneously could be explained by the movement from Stage I directly to Stage III because of low costs of fertility regulation (resulting from easily available information or a lack of taboos) or a sharp decline in C^d (resulting from a change in tastes for children, an increase in the relative price of children, or higher material aspirations).

II.2 APPLYING THE THEORETICAL MODEL TO THE U.S. EXPERIENCE

It is not immediately apparent where the United States in the nineteenth century fits into the scheme described above. The fact that fertility was declining since at least 1800 seems to indicate that the third stage of development had been reached. It is unlikely, however, that a widespread decline in mortality had occurred before the latter part of the century. The relevant question therefore is: Why did fertility decline in the face of stable mortality conditions?

From the general model, fertility could decline if one of two situations had occurred:

A. The United States was in Stage I with C^d greater than C^n (causing C to be equal to C^n) and C^n was declining, or,
B. C^d was less than C^n.

Given the historical record of U.S. mortality, situation A can be dismissed.[7] The evidence thus points to the second situation in which a potential excess supply of surviving children existed, thereby creating the motivation to restrict fertility.

Even if it were agreed that situation B occurred, it is still not completely clear why C decreased over time. Some possibilities are:

B.1. The natural supply of children was increasing, leading to an increase in the number of unwanted children. The disutility associated with unrestricted fertility therefore increased.
B.2. The costs of fertility regulation were decreasing.
B.3. The demand for children was decreasing, leading to an increase in the number of unwanted children. The disutility associated with unrestricted fertility therefore increased.

Hypothesis B.1 can be ruled out because of the apparent lack of improvement in mortality or fecundity conditions during this period. Similarly, it is unlikely that B.2 was an important explanatory factor in the fertility decline since there is little evidence that the costs of regulating fertility in the United States had changed significantly during the nineteenth century.[8] It thus appears that the fertility experience of the United States can be attributed for the most part to the third hypothesis—a decline in the demand for children had created the motivation to adopt fertility control techniques.

Changes in any argument of the demand function could have been responsible for the decline in demand over time. For example, an increase in the relative price of children may have occurred. This would be consistent with one popular hypothesis, that urbanization and industrialization had made children relatively more costly by increasing their direct and indirect costs while reducing their contribution to family income.[9] Moreover, urban growth increases the exposure to market goods which may produce a change in preferences from children to goods. While urbanization and industrialization are theoretically consistent with the decline in C^d, the data, however, do not support the hypothesis that these factors had been a dominant cause of the decline in nineteenth-century U.S. fertility.[10] Fertility rates experienced a large-scale decline while the United States remained largely rural and, moreover, rural fertility rates had declined at a faster rate. Thus, the key to understanding the overall decline in U.S. fertility lies in explaining the rural decline.[11]

It is possible that changes in the factors mentioned above, tastes and relative prices, might have affected rural fertility. While the lack of data prevents an empirical time-series analysis, there is little evidence of changes in attitudes, children's contribution to family income, or in the direct or the indirect costs of raising children.[12]

Another determinant of the demand for children, income, may have played a role in decreasing the demand for children, however. Children are assumed to be "normal goods," and therefore a decrease in rural income could account for a decline in C^d. Similarly, prospective income may be weighed against some minimum desired income level that must be achieved before children are demanded. An increase in the minimum desired income level relative to prospective income would lead to a decrease in the demand for children. Changes in prospective or minimum desired income may underlie the success of the one group of variables, measures of the availability of land, which have been successful in explaining changes in fertility over time and variations at a given time.

Land availability proxies have been tested in a variety of studies and a strong relationship between fertility and land availability has been established at several levels of aggregation (national, state, country, and household).[13] Yet there is no clear consensus concerning what this variable represents. Returning to the general fertility model, changes in land availability are unlikely to affect C^n or CFR but may lead to changes in C^d that are consistent with explanation B.3. As land availability is reduced, preferences may shift away from children, the relative price of children may increase, or the ratio of prospective to minimum desired income may fall. The third possibility appears the most likely.[14]

In rural areas, farmland is typically the main source of income and therefore, earning prospects depend largely on farm characteristics. As unused farmland becomes more scarce, it seems likely that it would become increasingly costly to acquire a workable farm.[15] Married couples who lived as part of an extended family may have decreased their demand for children as the possibility of setting up their own farms decreased, thereby causing a decline in expected income and the expectation of a tighter budget constraint.[16] Further, there is some evidence that areas with little available land (older farm areas) contained farms that had lower rates of return on capital, reflecting not only the higher initial investment in farmland but also the decline in the price of farm products and the decline in the arability of the land resulting from its overuse.[17]

Easterlin's bequest hypothesis ties changes in the price and profitability of land associated with changes in its availability to variations in the ratio of prospective to minimum income.[18] He assumes that, in the northern states, parents wish to supply each of their children with at least as good a chance for financial success in their lives as they themselves had received upon reaching the point where they had left their own parents' household.[19] Within the framework of the general fertility model, the desire to provide farmland (or, the funds to purchase farmland) can be treated as a component of the minimum desired income variable. As the price of farmland increased with the decrease in the amount of available land, it became more costly to provide nearby farms to children and, therefore, minimum desired income rose.[20] This factor is magnified by the decline in the rate of return on capital accompanying the decline in land availability. Thus, the decline in prospective income and the increase in minimum desired income may explain the apparent decline in the demand for children associated with a decrease in the availability of land.

It is interesting to examine whether there have been parallels to the U.S. case in the historical experiences of other nations. In the literature dealing with the study of inheritance procedures, the distinction is often made between two types of systems: impartibility, where land is transferred from one generation to another without being divided, and partibility, where the land is divided into a number of separate farms.[21] The first system is usually characterized by primogeniture: a single heir (often the oldest son) is given all of the parents' land while the rest of the children may be left to fend for themselves.[22] Multigeniture is practiced under a system of partibility that is based on the equal division of land among all children. In order to provide for each child, the family property is broken up, possibly leading to the formation of many small farms, none of which is of sufficient size to be economically viable.[23]

In Easterlin's model, the practice of providing for all children was adopted from the partible system, usually without the breakdown of family property into smaller units.[24] Concern with transfering farms which were large enough to capture economies of scale was not limited to the United States. Le Play, writing about nineteenth century France, discussed the idea that the demand for children had been decreasing as the desire for parents to maintain some minimum farm size conflicted with the partibility provision of the Civil Code.[25] Berkner and Mendels, in their analysis of inheritance practices in Western Europe during the eighteenth and nineteenth centuries, similarly suggested that higher inheritance costs had led to a decline in the demand for children in order to minimize the probability that the desired number of heirs would be exceeded.[26]

II.3 CONCLUSION

It has been established that the likely cause of the unusual decline in U.S. fertility during a period when mortality conditions were apparently stable was a decrease in the demand for children. A theoretical justification for a link between a fall in the desired number of children and a decrease in the availability of land has been provided as the relationship between land scarcity and inheritance practices has been explored. Chapter III examines the success of land availability variables in explaining the decline in fertility rates over time and across states and the resulting equations are used to produce a panel of crude birth rate predictions. These equations ultimately constitute a key component of the settlement model.

NOTES AND REFERENCES

1. Chapters II and III draw heavily on material presented in Morton Owen Schapiro, "Land Availability and Fertility in the United States, 1760–1870," *Journal of Economic History,* 42 (Sept. 1982), 577–600, although the present analysis deals with a slightly later period and extends the earlier discussion in a number of instances.

2. The decline in fertility rates during the nineteenth century is well documented. Early studies by Ezra C. Seaman, *Essays on the Progress of Nations* (New York, 1853); George Tucker, *Progress of the United States in Population and Wealth in Fifty Years* (New York, 1855); John S. Billings, "The Diminishing Birth Rate in the United States," *Forum,* 15 (June 1893), 470–75, and Walter F. Willcox, "The Change in the Proportion of Children in the United States and in the Birth Rate in France During the Nineteenth Century," *Publications of the American Statistical Association,* 12 (March 1911), 491–95, have been reinforced by more recent work by Warren S. Thompson and P, K. Whelpton, *Population Trends in the United States* (New York, 1933); Wilson H. Grabill, Clyde V. Kiser, and P. K. Whelpton, *The Fertility of American Women* (New York, 1958); Yasukichi Yasuba, *Birth Rates of the White Population in the United States, 1800–1860* (Baltimore, 1962); Ansley J. Coale and Melvin Zelnik, *New Estimates of Fertility and Population in the United States* (Princeton, 1963); and Colin Forster and G. S. L. Tucker, *Economic Opportunity and White American Fertility Ratios: 1800–1860* (New Haven, 1972).

3. In an extensive study of Massachusetts (a state with an early system of recording both births and deaths), Maris A. Vinovskis, "A Multivariate Regression Analysis of Fertility Differentials Among Massachusetts Townships and Regions in 1860," in *Historical Studies of Changing Fertility,* Charles Tilly, ed., (Princeton, 1978), has shown that the birth rate had declined during the period from 1790 to 1860 while the death rate remained stable. Yasuba, *Birth Rates;* Edward Meeker, "The Improving Health of the United States, 1850–1915," *Explorations in Economic History,* 9 (Summer 1972), 353–73; and Michael R. Haines, "The Use of Model Life Tables to Estimate Mortality for the United States in the Late Nineteenth Century," *Demography,* 16 (May 1979), 289–312, agreed that it is unlikely that a sustained decline in mortality rates had occurred in the United States before about 1880.

4. Etienne van de Walle, "Alone in Europe: The French Fertility Decline Until 1850," in *Historical Studies,* Tilly, ed., in a study of France; John E. Knodel, *The Decline of Fertility in Germany* (Princeton, 1974), in a study of

Germany; and Paul Demeny, "Early Fertility Decline in Austria-Hungary: A Lesson in Demographic Transition," *Daedalus,* 97 (Spring 1968), 502–22, in a study of Austria-Hungary, have shown instances where a concurrent decline in fertility and mortality had apparently occurred and have raised the possibility of a fertility decline preceding a mortality decline. Paul C. Matthiesson and James C. McCann, "The Role of Mortality in the European Fertility Transition: Aggregate-Level Relations," in *The Effects of Infant and Child Mortality on Fertility,* Samuel H. Preston, ed., (New York, 1978), provide evidence that the typical European experience had been characterized by a fertility decline following the decline in mortality.

5. Richard A. Easterlin, "The Economics and Sociology of Fertility: A Synthesis," in *Historical Studies,* Tilly, ed., and "An Economic Framework for Fertility Analysis," *Studies in Family Planning,* 6 (March 1975), 54–63.

6. Easterlin, "An Economic Framework," proposes several scenarios for fertility determination, one of which is presented in Figure II.1.

7. Although both Yasuba, *Birth Rates,* and Meeker, "The Improving Health," discuss the possibility that mortality actually rose during the decades around the middle of the nineteenth century, this increase (which could have caused C^n to decline) was thought to have been small and short-lived. Another factor which would have led to a decline in natural fertility would be a decline in fecundity due, possibly, to longer lactation periods. Again, this does not appear to have taken place during this time.

8. See Michael A. La Sorte, "Nineteenth Century Family Planning Practices," *The Journal of Psychohistory,* 4 (Fall 1976), 163–83.

9. See J. Potter, "The Growth of Population in America, 1700–1860," in *Population in History,* D. V. Glass and D. E. C. Eversley, eds. (London, 1965).

10. Grabill, Kiser, and Whelpton, *Fertility,* have shown that the decline in rural fertility accounted for 56% of the decline in U.S. fertility during the period 1810–1940. Yasuba, *Birth Rates,* and Forster and Tucker, *Economic Opportunity,* agree that it is unlikely that urbanization played a dominant role in explaining the decline in fertility during the first half of the nineteenth century. In fact, Forster and Tucker attribute 78% of the fertility decline during the period 1810–1840 and 74% of the fertility decline during the period 1840–1860 to the decline in rural birth rates.

11. The only way in which urbanization-industrialization could have been responsible for the rural fertility decline would have been if the lower urban birth rates had somehow been diffused into the countryside, and, as Forster and Tucker, *Economic Opportunity,* pointed out, this is highly unlikely, particularly since there is no evidence showing that urban fertility decreased before rural fertility.

12. While time-series data are scarce, cross-sectional data do exist. In a study of rural households in 16 northern states in 1860, Richard A. Easterlin, George Alter, and Gretchen A. Condran, "Farms and Farm Families in Old and New Areas: The Northern United States in 1860," in *Family and Population in Nineteenth-Century America,* Tamara K. Hareven and Maris A. Vinovskis, eds., (Princeton, 1978), find that these variables cannot explain the variation in fertility rates.

13. As early as 1855, Tucker, *Progress of the United States,* discusses the inverse relationship between fertility and a variant of the land availability variable, population density. Yasuba, *Birth Rates,* after a detailed analysis of the decline in rural fertility during the period 1800–1860, concludes that the availability of land was a major determinant of this decline. Forster and Tucker, *Economic Opportunity,* use a more sophisticated methodology and confirm Yasuba's findings. On a more disaggregated level, Don R. Leet, "Interrelations of Population Density, Urbanization, Literacy, and Fertility," *Explorations in Economic History,* 14 (Oct. 1977), 388–401; Easterlin, Alter, and Condran, "Farms and Farm Families"; and, for Canada, R. M. McInnis, "Birth Rates and Land Availability in North America in the Nineteenth Century, With Special Reference to Ontario," mimeographed (Queen's University, 1972) and "Childbearing and Land Availability: Some Evidence From Individual Household Data," in *Population Patterns in the Past,* Ronald Demos Lee, ed., (New York, 1977), also find that land availability had been a critical factor in accounting for variations in fertility. In his ambitious study of U.S. fertility patterns since the Civil War, Peter Lindert, *Fertility and Scarcity in America* (Princeton, 1978), similarly found that the availability of land encouraged marriage and fertility. Nevertheless, there have been several studies challenging the significance of land availability in explaining the decline in U.S. fertility. For example, for a critical discussion of Forster and Tucker, see Maris A. Vinovskis, "Socioeconomic Determinants of Interstate Fertility Differentials in the United States in 1850 and 1860," *Journal of Interdisciplinary History,* 3 (Winter 1976), pp. 375–98, and his more recent book, *Fertility in Massachusetts from the Revolution to the Civil War,* (New York, 1981). Unfortunately, the lack of panel data on education and other variables that Vinovskis used as alternatives to land availability prevented their inclusion in the empirical analysis that follows.

14. Easterlin, Alter, and Condran, "Farms and Farm Families," find no evidence that the degree of settlement affected the child's contribution to family income or the opportunity cost of a wife's time.

15. Leet, "Interrelations," examines the relationship between the availability of land and farm prices in Ohio during the middle part of the nineteenth century and finds that they were inversely correlated.

16. In addition, Yasuba, *Birth Rates,* finds that changes in marital customs (an increase in the age at first marriage and a decrease in the proportion married) played a significant role in reducing fertility during the first half of the nineteenth century. This may reflect the delay or cancellation of marriages due to poor income prospects associated with the decline in the availability of land. While, for some, rural-urban migration was an alternative to remaining on the farm, low levels of urbanization made this an unlikely possibility during the early part of the period in question. The role of urbanization is examined empirically in Section VI.3.

17. These factors are discussed in Clarence H. Danhof, *Change in Agriculture: The Northern United States, 1820–1870* (Cambridge, 1969); Neil Adams McNall, *An Agricultural History of the Genesee Valley 1790–1860* (Philadelphia, 1952); Richard A. Easterlin, "Farm Production and Income in Old and New

Areas at Mid-Century," in *Essays in Nineteenth Century Economic History: The Old Northwest,* Richard K. Vedder and David C. Klingaman, eds. (Athens, Ohio, 1975); and Leet, "Interrelations." Richard A. Easterlin, "Population Change and Farm Settlement in the Northern United States," *Journal of Economic History,* 36 (March 1976), 45–75, has conjectured that the reason for the persistence of unequal returns between older and newer areas stemmed from the nonpecuniary advantages to those residing in more densely settled (older) areas.

18. Easterlin, "Population Change."

19. In a rural area, this means providing either farmland itself or the funds needed to purchase farmland that supplied the same or better earning prospects as the farmland that the parents had inherited or had otherwise come into possession of when they had first set up their own farms. There have been many references to the desire of parents in rural areas to provide farms for their children. Philip J. Greven, Jr., *Four Generations: Population, Land and Family in Colonial Andover, Massachusetts* (Ithaca, 1970), in a study of Andover, Massachusetts during the seventeenth and eighteenth centuries found that it was common practice for parents to provide their children with land or the funds to purchase land on which to start their own farms. Allan G. Bogue, *From Prairie to Corn Belt* (Chicago, 1963), in a study of farming in Illinois and Iowa during the nineteenth century; and Danhof, *Change in Agriculture,* writing about the Northern United States during the middle of the nineteenth century, found similar evidence. Finally, W. J. Spillman, "The Agricultural Ladder," *American Economic Review,* Supplement, 9 (March 1919), 170–79, writing about the early 1900s, found that a minimum of 64% of farm owners had acquired farms with the aid of their families. It is safe to assume that this percentage had been even higher during an earlier period. Based on testimony of this type, Easterlin, "Population Change," concluded that family assistance with respect to the purchase of farms by children appeared to have been a common practice within the northern United States during the nineteenth century. The relationship between land availability, inheritance practices and the demand for children is examined further in Lee J. Alston and Morton Owen Schapiro, "Inheritance Laws Across Colonies: Causes and Consequences," *Journal of Economic History,* 44 (June 1984), 277–287.

20. It may have been true that relatively inexpensive farmland was once available in less settled areas, but these areas were generally far from the site of the parents' farm and the desire to keep the family together would have prevented the purchase of this farmland.

21. See, for example, Lutz K. Berkner and Franklin F. Mendels, "Inheritance Systems, Family Structure and Demographic Patterns in Western Europe, 1700–1900," in *Historical Studies,* Tilly, ed., and Lutz K. Berkner, "Peasant Household Organization and Demographic Change in Lower Saxony (1689–1766)," in *Population Patterns,* Lee, ed.

22. This system is usually expected to lead to a number of demographic effects including high levels of out-migration, a late mean age at first marriage, a relatively low proportion married, and the continuation of an ex-

tended family household organization. This is true when the bulk of the value of the parents' estate consists of farmland and, therefore, there are few additional assets that could be distributed among the other children. However, Alston and Schapiro, "Inheritance Laws," argue that the key to the demographic impact of primogeniture is the availability of land since, when land is easily available, it is possible for younger children to marry and to set up farms of their own. Thus, primogeniture and available land may lead to rapid population growth.

23. The demographic manifestations of this system are typically thought to be the opposite of impartibility: little out-migration, early marriages, and a breakdown in extended families. Yet, Alston and Schapiro, "Inheritance Laws," argue that multigeniture and land scarcity may lead to slow population growth as prior fragmentation of farms creates economic pressures to limit fertility. This is particularly true when there is a bequest motive in which parents desire to transfer a farm of some minimum efficient size.

24. Unless family farms were large enough to subdivide into smaller farms, each with a minimum size (or income generating potential) at least as large as the parents' original farm, impartibility would be prevalent.

25. Frederic LePlay, *L'Organization de la Famille* (Paris, 1871).

26. Berkner and Mendels, "Inheritance Systems."

Chapter III

A Fertility Model

In this chapter, a land availability model of fertility is specified and estimated (III.1), the accuracy of its predictions is examined (III.2), rate of natural increase predictions are made (III.3) and conclusions are presented (III.4). Finally, an appendix (III.5) contains the derivation of adjustment factors used in calculating birth rate estimates.

III.1 SPECIFICATION AND ESTIMATION OF THE MODEL

The time period under examination coincides with the century or so when fertility rates declined while mortality rates apparently remained stable. The period beginning with the decade 1790–1800 and concluding with the decade 1890–1900 thus is considered.

As is the case throughout the study, the sample set consists of the rural population of 23 northern states. The concentration on rural areas reflects the importance of the rural fertility decline in the overall U.S. experience.[1] The states were selected for reasons of data availability as well as the desire to isolate a fairly homogenous area, thereby increasing the probability that the observed variation in fertility among the states can be explained by certain independent variables, rather than as being the result of idiosyncratic economic and social structures within specific states. Thus, all 23 states are located in the northern part of the country, while states with major institutional differentials (such as the southern states where slavery played an important role) or states which relied heavily on specific rural activities (such as the western states where mining accounted for a significant part of the rural economy) were excluded. The states are: Maine, New Hampshire, Vermont, Massachusetts, Rhode Island, Connecticut, New York, New Jersey, Pennsylvania, Delaware, Maryland, Ohio, Indiana, Illinois, Michigan, Wisconsin, Minnesota, Iowa, Missouri, North Dakota, South Dakota, Nebraska, and Kansas. Since they are among the first states to be settled within the United States, they correspond nicely with those examined in other studies of early fertility changes. Finally, as in these other studies, the sample population used in estimating the fertility model excludes non-whites (a group which comprised a small percentage of the population in the rural north during this time), thereby assuring the comparability of results.

The independent variables measure land availability. As previously discussed, these variables have been successful in other studies and their ability to explain the cross-sectional and time-series variation in fertility rates will be examined below. These studies have used a variety of land availability proxies. Early work relied on population density variables but these may lead to ambiguous results.[2] Other studies have attempted to compute the amount of land in use at a certain date as a proportion of the maximum amount of land that was potentially usable. There are problems with the denominator of this ratio, however, since technological change and other factors affect the amount of land suitable for cultivation at any given time. For example, the adoption of the number of arable acres at some future date may lead to an overestimate of the availability of land since at least some of the land under cultivation in the future would not have been suitable for farming at the earlier date. This problem affected the work of Yasuba, who used the 1949 cropland acreage as the denominator of his land availability variable.[3] Forster and Tucker, seeking to improve on Yasuba's measure, used the number of farms recorded at three alternative dates—1850, 1860, and 1880—as their denominator.[4] A variety of ways to estimate the numerator of the land availability measure also exist, ranging from the use of the amount of ever-improved land at a given time to, in the case of Forster and Tucker, the number of adults.

The land availability measures used below are slightly modified versions of those found in previous studies. As described earlier, the first of the land availability variables measures the degree of scarcity within each state and is referred to as the internal density measure. Specifically, the numerator is the rural population of state s at time t ($RP_{s,t}$) while the denominator is the maximum rural population of state s (MRP_s). The denominator is calculated by examining the data on rural population by state and taking the first clear peak in these figures (after a period of stabilization or limited decline, a second peak often followed with the spread of the automobile). The maximum rural value typically occurred in the late nineteenth or early twentieth century, thereby coming after the first of Forster and Tucker's measures, but in all cases the date was earlier than the time chosen by Yasuba.[5] The other land availability variable, referred to as the total density measure, is a calculation of the scarcity of land in all of the states at a given time. This variable is computed by taking the total rural population at time t for all of the states ($\Sigma_s RP_{s,t}$) and dividing this number by the total maximum rural population for all of the states ($\Sigma_s MRP_s$).[6]

In theory, a number of different variables can be used to measure the dependent variable, the level of fertility. In the case of the nineteenth century United States, however, the choice is severely restricted by the data. The age enumeration found in each census starting in 1800 allows for the calculation of various types of child ratios, but the absence of birth data prevents the direct estimation of a measure such as the crude birth rate (the number of births per one thousand persons). Thus the measure of fertility that has been used most often in previous studies has been some type of child-woman ratio or, more crudely, a child-population ratio. Following this approach, the basic fertility measure used in the fertility model is the number of children aged 0 to 9, C, per 1,000 women aged 16 to 44, W (referred to as the birth ratio). Since the ultimate goal of this model is to estimate the rural crude birth rate by state and by decade, the estimation of a fertility equation that uses the birth ratio as the dependent variable is only the first step in the analysis.

Data on the rural white birth ratio unfortunately exist only for the period 1800–1840. Forster and Tucker calculated these figures by looking at U.S. Census data and deleting the urban population of townships for each age group in each state.[7] They were unable to continue this process after 1840 because, starting with the 1850 census, there were no longer any data on the age distribution at the township level. It would have been possible to have deleted the urban population of counties but this would have produced a rural birth ratio series that would not have been comparable with the estimates for the preceding period. The data on the dependent variable are therefore available for each of the five decade years from 1800 to 1840 rather than for the entire period.[8] Ideally, the period for which an equation is expected to make predictions corresponds with the period in which the data used in the estimation of the equation were drawn. This often is not the case, however (for example, a forecasting equation necessarily predicts outside of the sample period). The success of the birth ratio equation in accurately forecasting for the entire period (or at least ensuring that the forecasts for the period before 1800 and after 1840 be as accurate as those for the period 1800–1840) relies on the maintenance of a stable relationship between the dependent and independent variables along with a properly specified equation. In the absence of either a shift in the parameters or changes in omitted variables, no reason exists to anticipate any problems arising from the limited sample.

The birth ratio equation was estimated using a procedure that took advantage of the information given by the particular nature of the data set. The same units are followed over time and, therefore, the data set is a panel, with time-series and cross-sectional variation. For this type of data set, an ordinary least-squares regression procedure may not be the best estimation technique. The error-components method, a generalized least-squares procedure, offers an increase in efficiency by accounting for the existence of cross-sectional and time-series errors.[9] Specifically, the residual error, $r_{s,t}$ is assumed to be randomly distributed and can be decomposed into three components of variation: v_s, the cross-sectional error component; e_t, the time-series error component; and $w_{s,t}$ the combined error component; all independently distributed with zero means and variances $\sigma_v^2 \geq 0$, $\sigma_e^2 \geq 0$, and $\sigma_w^2 > 0$. The data set used in the regression procedure consisted of 65 observations.[10]

Lagged values of the independent variables were used since the fertility measure is the number of children aged 0 to 9, and, therefore, the birth ratio at time t reflects the number of births during the period from t-10 to t. Thus, land availability conditions at time t-10 were used to predict the birth ratio at time t. The bequest hypothesis considers the internal density measure to be a proxy for the ability of parents to provide farms for their children within nearby areas while the total density measure reflects the ability to provide farms anywhere within the 23-state area. Since Easterlin assumed that there was a desire to keep the family living within the same general vicinity, this would imply that the internal density measure would be more successful in explaining the variation in fertility than would the other land availability measure.[11] In any case, the coefficient of each variable is expected to be negative, indicating that a decline in the amount of available land (an increase in either of the variables) leads to lower fertility.

Table III.1 presents the results of the generalized least-squares error-components regression procedure. The regression coefficients were significant at the highest conventional test levels and each had the "correct" sign. The testing of alternative specifications of the birth ratio equation indicated that the internal density measure played a larger role in explaining changes in

Table III.1. The Determinants of the Birth Ratio, Pooled Regression Results

Dependent Variable	*Constant*	*Independent Variables*	
		$RP_{s,t-10}/MRP_s$	$\Sigma_s RP_{s,t-10}/\Sigma_s MRP_s$
$(1000C/W)_{s,t}$	2268.03 (46.7)[a]	−978.44 (10.7)[a]	−819.15 (3.3)[a]

Note: Absolute values of t-statistics are in parentheses.
[a]Significant at the 99% level.

C is the number of children aged 0 to 9. W is the number of women aged 16 to 44. RP is the size of the rural population. MRP is the size of the maximum rural population. A generalized least-squares error-components regression procedure was used.

Source: See text.

fertility than the total density measure, thereby being consistent with the prediction of the bequest theory.[12]

The accuracy of predictions outside of the sample set (before 1800 and after 1850) cannot be systematically evaluated (if data had been available for these decades, they would have been used in the estimation of the equation). A residual check, however, demonstrated that the equation was quite accurate in predicting the birth ratio during the sample period.[13]

The birth ratio is just one component of a more general fertility variable, the crude birth rate. Predictions of the crude birth rate are of direct interest since it is possible to compare these estimates with those generated in a number of other studies. The relationship between a variant of the crude birth rate and the birth ratio can be seen in the following equation:

$$(1000C/P)_{s,t} = (1000C/W)_{s,t} \cdot (1000W/P)_{s,t} \cdot 1/1000 \qquad (1)$$

where P is the population, C is the number of children aged 0 to 9 and W is the number of women aged 16 to 44. The reason that this is not a true crude birth rate equation is that the dependent variable is not the number of births per thousand people, but, instead, is the number of children. In any case, the birth ratio must be multiplied by the proportion of women aged 16 to 44 in the population (henceforth referred to as the proportion of reproductive females). Thus it is clear that the crude birth rate is determined by two separate variables and, therefore, the link between fertility and land availability can be either through the birth ratio or through the proportion of reproductive females.

It is theoretically possible that changes in the availability of land affect the sex composition of the population. Older, more densely settled areas are more likely to have a substantial number of females than less settled areas since, traditionally, males were the first to migrate to frontier areas.[14] Therefore, an increase in the value of the internal density measure should induce greater in-migration of females, increasing the proportion of reproductive females in the population. In addition, an increase in the settlement level of the entire area would be expected to lead to a higher proportion of reproductive females in any state regardless of its own land availability situation since the neighboring states would be more likely to have a substantial number of females, thereby decreasing the cost of migrating from highly settled areas to the frontier and, at the same time, making unsettled states less isolated and dangerous. Thus the total density measure is also assumed to be positively related to the proportion-of-reproductive-females variable.

The data set for the dependent variable is limited by two factors. As in the case of the birth ratio, the lack of age enumeration information before 1800 prevents the calculation of a value for the decade 1790–1800. In addition, available data do not differentiate between rural or urban residence. This could cause problems since the proportion of reproductive females is expected to be higher in states that had a higher degree of urbanization. The relative unimportance of urbanization for most states at most of the dates being considered, however, limits the extent of the urbanization bias.[15]

The proportion-of-reproductive-females equation was estimated using the same pooling procedure based on the error-components method as was used in the estimation of the birth ratio equation and, therefore, the error assumptions detailed above also apply here. Once again, a ten year lag on the independent variables was used, reflecting the lag between changes in settlement level and the in-migration of females. The data set used in the regression procedure consisted of 104 observations (13 states at 8 different dates).

Table III.2 presents the results of the generalized least-squares error-components regression procedure. Each inde-

Table III.2. The Determinants of the Proportion of Reproductive Females, Pooled Regression Results

Dependent Variable	*Constant*	*Independent Variables*	
		$RP_{s,t-10}/MRP_s$	$\Sigma_s RP_{s,t-10}/\Sigma_s MRP_s$
$(1000W/P)_{s,t}$	180.12 (34.0)[a]	29.21 (5.2)[a]	49.14 (3.3)[a]

Note: Absolute values of t-statistics are in parentheses.
[a]Significant at the 99% level.

W is the number of women aged 16 to 44. P is the size of the entire population. RP is the size of the rural population. MRP is the size of the maximum rural population.

A generalized least-squares error-components regression procedure was used.

Source: See text.

pendent variable was significant and had the expected sign as higher levels of settlement (larger values for the density variables) led to an increase in the proportion of the population consisting of females aged 16 to 44.[16] An analysis of the residuals showed that the equation was able to predict accurately the proportion of reproductive females during the sample period.[17]

Now that the equations that forecast the two major components of the crude birth rate have been estimated, the predictions from the two equations can be combined and, after a variety of adjustments have been made, a set of crude birth rate estimates can be produced. First, a crude birth rate equation must be specified.

There are two problems with the crude birth rate variant in Equation (1). The dependent variable considers the number of children rather than the number of births, and its values are measured at time t rather than for the decade lasting from t to t+10. The ideal fertility variable would be the crude birth rate for state s during the decade lasting from t to t+10, $CBR_{s,t \rightarrow t+10}$, which would represent the average annual number of births during the decade per one thousand people where the population is the average population during the decade. This variable can be approximated by using the mid-decade population and, therefore, the desired fertility variable is:

$$\left(1000 \sum_{t=1}^{10} B_{s,t}/10\right) \Big/ P_{s,t+5}$$

where B is the number of births.

In order to change Equation (1) so that the dependent variable is the crude birth rate, a number of adjustments must be made. First, the independent variables should be computed at time t+10 since the number of children aged 0 to 9 at t+10 reflects fertility in the preceding decade. After making this adjustment, the denominator of the proportion-of-reproductive-females variable is the population at t+10 rather than at t+5, thereby biasing the crude birth rate estimate downward when the population is growing. Thus, a population adjustment factor, $P_{s,t+10}/P_{s,t+5}$, must be used.

A more difficult problem arises from the need to estimate the average annual number of births from census information on the number of surviving children. The total number of births from t to t+10 is equal to the number of surviving children aged 0 to 9 at t+10 as recorded in census data, plus the number of children born in the relevant period who died, plus the number of children alive at t+10 who were not included in the census enumeration.[18] Thus,

$$\sum_{t=1}^{10} B_{s,t} = C_{s,t+10} + C_{s,t+10}(m_{s,t\rightarrow t+10}) + C_{s,t+10}(u_{s,t+10}) \qquad (2)$$

where m represents the mortality adjustment factor (the ratio of the number of children who died before t+10 to the number who survived and were counted) and u represents the child under-enumeration adjustment factor (the ratio of the number of children who were omitted from the census count to the number who were included). In addition, there will be less than complete enumeration for the population variable, $P_{s,t+5}$, so the adjusted population is equal to the recorded population plus the number omitted:

$$P_{as,t+5} = P_{s,t+5} + P_{s,t+5}(p_{s,t+5}) \qquad (3)$$

where $P_{as,t+5}$ is the adjusted population figure and p is the population under-enumeration adjustment figure. There is no need to adjust the numerator of the proportion-of-reproductive-females variable for either mortality or under-enumeration since this quantity is also the denominator of the birth ratio variable and therefore cancels out.

Modifying Equation (1) by incorporating all of the adjustment factors yields a crude birth rate equation:

$$\begin{aligned} CBR_{s,t\rightarrow t+10} &= \left(1000 \sum_{t=1}^{10} B_{s,t}/10\right) \Big/ P_{as,t+5} \\ &= (1000C/W)_{s,t+10} \\ &\quad \cdot (1 + m_{s,t\rightarrow t+10} + u_{s,t+10}) \\ &\quad \cdot (1000W/P)_{s,t+10} \cdot P_{s,t+10}/P_{s,t+5} \\ &\quad \cdot 1/(1 + p_{s,t+5}) \cdot 1/10{,}000. \end{aligned} \qquad (4)$$

After a variety of substitutions are made, the values of the adjustment factors can be computed, yielding the final version of the crude birth rate equation (see the Appendix to this chapter):

$$C\hat{B}R_{s,t\rightarrow t+10} = (1000\hat{C}/W)_{s,t+10}\cdot(1000\hat{W}/P)_{s,t+10}\cdot.000153. \quad (5)$$

The predictions of the birth-ratio and proportion-of-reproductive-females equations can now be used to estimate the rural crude birth rate for the white population of each state during each of the decades starting with 1790–1800 and ending with 1890–1900.

III.2 ANALYSIS OF THE PREDICTIONS

Table III.3 presents the solution to Equation (5) for each state and each decade. Early predictions are extremely high relative to historical rates in Europe and to birth rates in the contemporary developing world. This reflects the unusual circumstances in the United States which led to fertility levels which have been virtually unmatched by other populations. While in almost all cases the predicted value for each of the states declines over time, the rate of decrease varies directly with the date of settlement as the predicted crude birth rates for the newer states tend to decline at a rate almost twice as fast as that of the older states. For example, it takes six or more decades for the crude birth rate predictions for most of the 13 states during the decade starting in 1790 to decline by one-third. The comparable figure for most of the newer states was in the three decade to four decade range. An examination of other estimates of the crude birth rate can provide an indication of the accuracy of these predictions.

Table III.4 presents crude birth rate estimates from a variety of sources along with a weighted average of the state predictions by decade from the fertility model. There are some questions that must be answered before these numbers can be compared. While the fertility model examines a subset of states, the other studies generally examine all of the states. In addition, the fertility model deals exclusively with rural areas while the

Table III.3. Predicted Rural White Crude Birth Rate by State, from the Decade 1790–1800 to the Decade 1890–1900

State	*1790–1800*	*1800–1810*	*1810–1820*	*1820–1830*	*1830–1840*	*1840–1850*	*1850–1860*	*1860–1870*	*1870–1880*	*1880–1890*	*1890–1900*
Maine	58.8	56.5	53.1	49.3	43.7	38.0	33.7	29.4	26.7	23.4	21.2
New Hampshire	51.7	47.5	44.1	40.4	37.3	35.5	32.4	30.5	26.7	23.4	21.2
Vermont	56.8	51.7	46.2	44.1	39.1	36.0	32.4	29.4	26.7	23.4	21.2
Massachusetts	48.4	46.7	45.2	42.9	40.7	37.0	32.8	29.4	26.7	23.4	21.2
Rhode Island	44.3	44.0	41.9	38.8	36.4	37.0	33.0	30.5	26.7	23.4	21.2
Connecticut	49.1	48.4	47.2	45.9	43.7	41.9	36.8	31.8	27.3	23.7	21.2
New York	59.5	57.7	54.4	50.3	44.9	39.5	34.2	29.4	26.7	23.4	21.2
New Jersey	55.7	54.4	52.8	50.7	48.4	45.7	40.4	34.9	29.2	26.0	22.2
Pennsylvania	59.3	58.2	56.7	54.5	52.1	48.2	43.5	38.6	34.1	27.5	23.0
Delaware	50.7	49.1	46.8	45.9	43.8	44.1	40.1	33.7	30.3	25.8	23.6
Maryland	52.3	52.0	50.9	49.6	48.1	46.7	43.5	38.3	34.4	27.5	26.1
Ohio	61.9	61.4	59.6	56.0	51.5	44.1	38.4	32.8	29.6	23.4	21.2
Indiana	61.9	62.0	61.5	59.5	56.2	50.6	44.7	37.0	30.9	24.8	22.2
Illinois		62.0	61.5	60.6	59.2	55.2	50.2	39.5	30.6	24.4	22.6
Michigan		62.0	61.4	60.9	60.3	56.8	53.0	45.9	38.0	29.1	24.0
Wisconsin					60.6	59.2	54.0	44.8	38.9	32.7	27.5
Minnesota						59.8	58.8	54.2	48.4	40.6	33.1
Iowa					60.6	59.2	56.3	47.8	38.4	29.1	24.3
Missouri			61.5	60.6	59.2	55.6	51.6	44.3	37.8	29.5	24.0
North Dakota							58.8	57.0	55.7	52.2	43.3
South Dakota							58.8	57.0	55.0	49.5	35.6
Nebraska							58.8	56.3	52.9	41.5	26.1
Kansas							58.8	55.2	48.8	31.1	21.2
Mean[a]	54.1	52.4	52.6	50.9	47.0	44.0	41.4	36.3	32.8	27.4	23.8

Note: [a]Weighted by population share.
Source: Equation (5).

Table III.4. Comparison of White Crude Birth Rate Estimates

	Total U.S.					Rural: 23 States
	(1)	(2)	(3)	(4)	(5)	(6)
Years	*Lotka*	*Blodget*	*Thompson and Whelpton*	*Yasuba*	*Coale and Zelnik*	*Fertility Model*
1790–1800	50.8					54.1
1790–1805		52–53				
1800			55.0	47.6–52.9		
1800–1810						52.4
1810			54.0	47.3–52.7		
1810–1820						52.6
1820			52.8	45.9–51.1		
1820–1830						50.9
1830			51.4	44.7–49.8		
1830–1840						47.0
1840			48.3	43.0–47.9		
1840–1850						44.0
1850			43.3	38.4–42.9		
1855					42.8	
1850–1860						41.4
1860			41.4	37.7–42.1	41.8	
1860–1870						36.3
1870			38.3		37.1	
1870–1880						32.8
1880			35.2		33.6	
1880–1890						27.4
1890			31.5		31.2	
1890–1900						23.8
1900			30.1		28.5	

Sources: (1) Alfred J. Lotka, "The Size of American Families in the Eighteenth Century and the Significance of the Emprical Constants in the Pearl-Reed Law of Population Growth," *Journal of the American Statistical Association,* New Series 22 (June 1927), p. 165; (2) Samuel Blodget, *Economica: A Statistical Manual for the United States of America* (Washington, D.C., 1806), p. 58; (3) Thompson and Whelpton, *Population Trends,* p. 263; (4) Yasuba, *Birth Rates,* p. 99; (5) Coale and Zelnik, *New Estimates,* p. 21; (6) Equation (5).

others are for rural and urban areas combined. It can be expected that fertility within the northern area had been somewhat lower than the national average because of the relatively high birth rates in the southern states.[19] On the other hand, the rural-total bias operates in the opposite direction since rural fertility was higher than urban fertility. Fortunately, there are data that can be used to determine which of the two adjustments is larger since it is not clear whether the crude birth rate estimates for all areas of all of the states should be adjusted upward or downward before being compared with the fertility model predictions.

Yasuba presented estimates for both the birth ratio and the proportion of reproductive females for states that are included in the northern subset as well as for additional states.[20] By calculating the ratio of the birth ratio in the northern area to the birth ratio for all of the states and then multiplying this number by the ratio of the proportion of reproductive females in the northern area to the proportion of reproductive females for all of the states, the difference between the crude birth rate in the northern area and the crude birth rate for all states can be computed.[21] In addition, estimates of the birth ratio for rural areas can be compared with those for rural and urban areas combined, and the magnitude of rural over total fertility can be estimated.[22] By multiplying the two conversion factors together, the ratio of the rural northern crude birth rate to the crude birth rate for all areas of all of the states can be computed. For the decade 1790–1800, this ratio was equal to .987. This implies that the crude birth rate for all areas of all of the states was 1.3 percent higher than the crude birth rate for rural areas of the northern states.

Because of the lack of rural township data after 1840, the decade lasting from 1830 to 1840 is the last for which the conversion factor can be calculated. For this decade, the crude birth rate for all areas of all of the states was 2.7% lower than the crude birth rate for rural areas of the northern states. A range of +1.3% to −2.7% indicates that the excess of the rural crude birth rate over the total crude birth rate was approximately equal to the excess of the crude birth rate for all of the states over the crude birth rate for the northern states. Data provided by Grabill, Kiser, and Whelpton produce a similar result.[23]

In total, it appears that the crude birth rate estimates for the white population living in all areas of all of the states, as presented in a number of studies, correspond reasonably well with the crude birth rate estimates for the white population living in rural areas of the northern states as predicted by the fertility model. An examination of Table III.4 shows that the forecasts of the fertility model are largely consistent with the results of these studies.[24] The crude birth rate prediction for the decade 1800–1810 (52.4) lies within the upper range of Yasuba's estimates over this period, as do the predictions for the decades 1810–1820 and 1820–1830. As mid-century is approached, the fertility model produces values that correspond with the middle range of Yasuba's estimates and are also comparable to the estimates of Thompson and Whelpton. After that date, the predictions of the fertility model approach and then fall beneath the lower range of the other estimates. It appears that the final few predictions are too low. This is likely due to the limited sample set used in estimating the birth ratio equation. As the crude birth rate approached the crude death rate, the relationship between land availability and the demand for children may have weakened, thereby limiting the continued reduction in birth rates. Thus, an equation estimated during a period when the crude birth rate was far in excess of the crude death rate is unable to take this factor into account. Alternatively, the link between land availability and fertility may have weakened by the end of the period as non-farm sources of rural earnings became more important. In any case, the predictions seem to be reasonable during most of the period under examination as the accuracy of the fertility model predictions is substantiated by estimates presented in several other studies, although the ultimate decline in birth rates is overstated.[25]

III.3 THE RATE OF NATURAL INCREASE

The crude birth rate model has now been specified and estimated and its predictions have been analyzed. It appears that a model based solely on the availability of land can be used to forecast the crude birth rate for the white population living in rural areas within a group of 23 northern states during the nineteenth century. Thus, a principal hypothesis from the second chapter, that differences in the availability of land were a major factor in accounting for the cross-sectional and time-series variation in the crude birth rate, has been substantiated. Now the rate of natural increase, a measure of population growth which is an important component of the settlement model presented in Chapter VI, can be computed.

The excess of births over deaths determines the rate of growth of the native population of a particular state. The rate of natural increase is a measure of this growth rate and its value can be predicted by taking the difference between the crude birth rate forecast and an estimate of the crude death rate:

$$\hat{RNI}_{s,t \rightarrow t+10} = (C\hat{B}R_{s,t \rightarrow t+10} - CDR_{s,t \rightarrow t+10})/100 \qquad (6)$$

where RNI is the rate of natural increase over the decade and CDR is the crude death rate. While the fertility model has produced a set of crude birth rate predictions by state and by decade, the values of the crude death rate will be given exogenously.

As described above, several studies of historical U.S. mortality have concluded that mortality had been relatively stable until the latter part of the nineteenth century (see, for example, Meeker and Yasuba).[26] Estimates of the value of the crude death rate before the start of the improvement in mortality have been produced by Meeker with a value of 23.1 for the white population during the middle part of the nineteenth century (1830–1860) and by Higgs and Kuznets who estimated that the crude death rate for the decade lasting from 1870 to 1880 was 23 and 19.9, respectively,[27] However, these estimates are for both urban and rural areas rather than for rural areas exclusively. Vinovskis, in an analysis of mortality in Massachusetts in 1860, concluded that the rural-urban mortality differential in that state had been relatively small, while Higgs, in a study of the entire United States, estimated that the rural crude death rate for the decade lasting from 1870 to 1880 had ranged somewhere between 21 and 23, only marginally less than his aggregate estimate.[28] Therefore, an overall value of 22 for the rural crude death rate seems reasonable.

Yet, the fact that the age distribution within the different states varies raises the possibility that the use of a single crude death rate value for all states may not be desirable. Specifically, states which are at low stages of development are expected to have a younger population profile than states which are more settled. Thus, states with lower internal density values may be expected to have lower crude death rates than states with higher internal density values. This proposition can be tested by applying mortality probabilities calculated from a model life table to the age distribution for different states as given by the 1860 census. The model life table which seems to best reflect mortality conditions in the rural United States during this period is Model West-Level 11 (this table assumes a life expectancy at birth of 45.0 years for females and 41.8 years for males).[29] The crude death rate estimates resulting from this procedure varied only slightly among the different states despite differences in the age distribution (all estimates were in the neighborhood of 20). Thus, the use of a single value of the crude death rate for rural areas of all the states is defensible, particularly since the severe lack of historical mortality data for the United States means that there are few, if any, viable alternatives.

The rate of natural increase predictions are, therefore, simply the estimates presented in Table III.3 minus 22. The pattern of change over time and the relationship among the states is repeated with the rate of natural increase predictions for each state showing a general downward trend over time and the rate of decrease being higher for the newer states.

III.4 CONCLUSION

It had earlier been argued that the likely cause of the decline in fertility in the face of stable mortality conditions was a decline in the demand for children. The fertility model tested whether this decline could be accounted for by changes in the availability of land, and the accuracy of its predictions demonstrates that land availability was a critical factor in explaining the variation in fertility rates across states and over time.

Studies of the effects of increasing land scarcity have often stressed its contribution to out-migration, a subject which will be examined in detail in Chapters V and VI. For example, Turner stated that changes in the availability of land induced westward migration and explained U.S. development:

> Year by year the farmers who lived on soil whose returns were diminished by unrotated crops were offered the virgin soil of the frontier at nominal prices. Their growing families demanded more lands, and these were dear. The competition of the unexhausted, cheap, and easily tilled prairie lands compelled the farmer either to go west and continue the exhaustion of the soil on a new frontier, or to adopt intensive culture.[30]

A reduction in the availability of land thus led to out-migration as the return on capital fell while the price of land remained high. These same factors, a decrease in farm profitability and an increase in the relative price of farmland, are assumed here to underlie the success of the land availability measures in the fertility model. Thus, in addition to inducing out-migration, the decline in the availability of land led to a decrease in fertility.

For Turner, the adverse conditions associated with the decline in available land in the East did not lead to the political, social, and economic upheaval experienced in a number of other nations because out-migration from the East to the frontier acted as a safety valve for eastern laborers and farmers. The decline in the demand for children seems to have served a similar function.[31] By restricting family size, the unfavorable effects of a decrease in the amount of available land were minimized. In order to examine whether the fertility decline was as important as westward migration in explaining the settlement pattern of the United States, a general dynamic model allowing for feedback between land availability, fertility, and migration is required. Chapter VI contains such a model which is used then in a more detailed quantitative analysis of the impacts of migration and of the decline in rural fertility on population growth and distribution. In this way, the notion of the "safety valve" in U.S. demographic history is further explored.

III.5 APPENDIX: CRUDE BIRTH RATE ADJUSTMENTS

Computing the values of the child and population under-enumeration factors and the population adjustment factor is fairly straightforward but the mortality adjustment factor is more complicated.

The number of children who would have been aged 0 to 9 at t+10 in the absence of mortality is equal to the number of children born at time t who died within ten years plus the number of children born at t+1 who died within nine years up to and including the number of children born at t+9 who died within one year. Therefore:

$$C_{s,t+10}(m_{s,t\rightarrow t+10}) = B_{s,t}({}_{10}q_0) + B_{s,t+1}({}_9q_0) + B_{s,t+2}({}_8q_0) + \ldots + B_{s,t+9}({}_1q_0) \quad \text{(A-1)}$$

where ${}_zq_x$ represents the probability of a person x years of age dying before age z. Equation (A-1) can be transformed into:

$$\begin{aligned} C_{s,t+10}(m_{s,t\rightarrow t+10}) = {} & B_{s,t}({}_{10}q_9 + {}_9q_8 + {}_8q_7 + \ldots + {}_1q_0) \\ & + B_{s,t+1}({}_9q_8 + {}_8q_7 + {}_7q_6 + \ldots + {}_1q_0) \\ & + B_{s,t+2}({}_8q_7 + {}_7q_6 + {}_6q_5 + \ldots + {}_1q_0) \\ & + \ldots + B_{s,t+9}({}_1q_0) \end{aligned} \quad \text{(A-2)}$$

since ${}_zq_x$ is equal to the probability of a person x years of age dying before age y plus the probability that the person would die between age y and age z (${}_zq_x = {}_zq_y + {}_yq_x$, where $x < y < z$).

Assuming that births are evenly distributed over the decade $\left(\text{that } \sum_{t=1}^{10} B_{s,t}/10 = B_{s,t} = B_{s,t+1} = \ldots = B_{s,t+9}\right)$, equation (A-2) becomes

$$C_{s,t+10}(m_{s,t\rightarrow t+10}) = \left(\sum_{t=1}^{10} B_{s,t}/10\right)(10_1q_0 + 9_2q_1 + 8_3q_2 + \ldots + {}_{10}q_9). \quad \text{(A-3)}$$

Substituting (A-3) into (2) yields:

$$\sum_{t=1}^{10} B_{s,t}/10 = C_{s,t+10}(1 + u_{s,t+10}) / (10 - (10_1q_0 + 9_2q_1 + 8_3q_2 + \ldots + {}_{10}q_9)). \quad \text{(A-4)}$$

The final form of the crude birth rate equation can now be derived:

$$\begin{aligned} CBR_{s,t\rightarrow t+10} &= \left(1000 \sum_{t=1}^{10} B_{s,t}/10\right) \Big/ P_{as,t+5} \\ &= (1000C/W)_{s,t+10} \cdot (1000W/P)_{s,t+10} \\ &\quad \cdot (1 + u_{s,t+10})/(1 + p_{s,t+5}) \\ &\quad \cdot P_{s,t+10}/P_{s,t+5} \\ &\quad \cdot 1/(10 - 10_1q_0 - 9_2q_1 - 8_3q_2 \\ &\quad - \ldots - {}_{10}q_9) \cdot 1/1000. \end{aligned} \qquad \text{(A-5)}$$

The original variant of the crude birth rate (Equation (1)) has been adjusted by three factors: a differential under-enumeration factor $((1 + u_{s,t+10})/(1 + p_{s,t+5}))$, a population adjustment factor $(P_{s,t+10}/P_{s,t+5})$ and a mortality adjustment for children $(1/(10 - 10_1q_0 - 9_2q_1 - 8_3q_2 - \ldots - {}_{10}q_9))$.

It is assumed that the third factor is the same for all states and for all decades. The first part of the assumption seems to be reasonable since only rural areas are being considered and it is unlikely that mortality conditions differed to any great extent within rural areas of the 23 states. The second part of the assumption relies on the evidence that shows that mortality rates had been stable until the second half of the nineteenth century. Therefore, any change in mortality conditions within rural areas is unlikely to have been very substantial during the period under examination.

The mortality probabilities can be calculated from the Model West-Level 11 life table used above.[32] Based on this table, the weighted sum of the qs was computed (2.45) and, from this value, a total adjustment value of .132 (1/7.55) was calculated.

The under-enumeration factor measures the degree that children were undercounted relative to the degree of under-enumeration for the entire population. If children had been under-enumerated by the same proportion as the rest of the population, there would be no need to adjust for under-enumeration (the factor would equal one and the crude birth rate estimate would remain unchanged). This does not appear to have been the case, however. There is little known about the extent of under-enumeration in early censuses, but it seems likely that young children had been subject to the largest enumeration errors. From Coale and Zelnik, it can be estimated that the enumeration error for children aged 0 to 9 during the latter part of the nineteenth century was in the 5–6% range.[33] A similar magnitude can be derived from the work of Grabill, Kiser, and Whelpton.[34] Thus, the numerator of the differential under-enumeration factor will be equal to 1.06 across states and over time.

The data concerning the denominator of the adjustment factor are even less complete. Since children are usually considered to be subject to the largest degree of under-enumeration, the average for the entire population should be somewhat less than 6%. Coale and Zelnik found, however, that the degree of under-enumeration for older persons was not consistently less than that of children, at least for twentieth century census data, and this implies that the enumeration error for the entire population was only slightly lower than the error which applies solely for children aged 0 to 9.[35] Therefore, the denominator of the differential under-enumeration factor will be equal to 1.04.

The final adjustment measure is the population adjustment factor. This variable takes account of the growth of the population between time t+5 and time t+10. Obviously, the value of this factor depends on how fast a state grows during a particular decade. The average growth rate of the rural population for the entire 23-state area by five year period (calculated by assuming that the population at time t+5 was a simple average of the population at time t and at time t+10) was, for the most part, within the 1.13 to 1.15 range, indicating an average population adjustment of about 14% during the entire period. The relative stability in the value of the population adjustment factor over most of the period implies that a single adjustment value may be used and, therefore, this factor will be equal to 1.14.

Numerical values have now been computed for all of the adjustment factors. Thus, Equation (A-5) becomes:

$$CBR_{s,t\rightarrow t+10} = \left(1000 \sum_{t=1}^{10} B_{s,t}/10\right) \Big/ P_{as,t+5}$$

$$= (1000C/W)_{s,t+10} \cdot (1000W/P)_{s,t+10}$$
$$\cdot 1.06/1.04 \cdot 1.14 \cdot .132 \cdot 1/1000. \quad \text{(A-6)}$$

NOTES AND REFERENCES

1. As discussed in Chapter II, the decline in rural fertility was more rapid than the decline in urban fertility and was responsible in large part for the total fertility decline. Moreover, the area under consideration was largely rural with the percentage of the population residing in rural areas equaling 91.1% in 1810, 85.9% in 1840, and 71.3% in 1870.

2. For example, Tucker, *Progress of the United States,* uses a population density measure as a proxy for land availability. Rapid urbanization during the latter part of the nineteenth century contributed to the rise in population density, however, and therefore weakened the link between density and the availability of land.

3. Yasuba, *Birth Rates.*

4. Forster and Tucker, *Economic Opportunity.*

5. The earliest maximum was reached in 1830 (Rhode Island) and the latest was reached in 1930 (North Dakota, South Dakota, and Nebraska). The median date was between 1890 and 1900.

6. See Tables I.1 and I.2 for the values of the total and internal density measures, respectively.

7. Forster and Tucker, *Economic Opportunity.*

8. There is no way to calculate the birth ratio by state before 1800 because the 1800 census contained the first age enumeration data.

9. W. A. Fuller and G. E. Battese, "Estimation of Linear Models with Crossed-Error Structure," *Journal of Econometrics,* 2 (May 1974), 67–78, present a technical discussion of this method. Robert S. Pindyck and Daniel L. Rubinfeld, *Economic Models and Economic Forecasts* (New York, 1976), pp. 202–11, have a more general discussion of pooling cross-section and time-series data.

10. A complete set of data for each state was needed. Therefore, data for the first thirteen states listed in Table III.3 for the dates 1800, 1810, 1820, 1830, and 1840 were used.

11. The total density measure at each date is the same for all states and, therefore, it may have the properties of a time trend. If, for example, there were a change in tastes over time, this variable could capture the shift in preferences away from children. Similarly, if the population were aging (leading to a decline in natural fertility) or immigration were increasing (and immigrants had lower fertility than native Americans), then the total density measure would take account of these factors. Yet, these and other factors that potentially could have altered the level of fertility appear to have had little effect during the nineteenth century, and the substitution of a time trend for the total density measure produced inferior results. It is thus reasonable to assume that changes in the total density measure represent changes in the ability to acquire farmland, which affect the demand for children.

12. While there are problems with the calculation and interpretation of a value of R^2 that arise when using this regression procedure, an ordinary least-squares technique produces an R^2 of .87, indicating that a substantial part of the variation has been explained.

13. Of the 65 cases that comprised the sample set, 97% had residuals less than or equal to 15% of the actual values, while 88% had residuals less than or equal to 10% of the actual values.

14. Easterlin, Alter, and Condran, "Farms and Farm Families," showed that the ratio of males aged 15 and over to females aged 15 and over was 25% higher in their least settled farm area compared with their most developed area in 1860.

15. It would be possible to estimate the proportion of reproductive females equation using only observations starting in 1800 and lasting until the middle part of the nineteenth century when the extent of urbanization was very small. But, even in 1870, the end of the sample period, over 70 percent of the total population lived in rural areas. These data are presented in Yasuba, *Birth Rates,* pp. 62–63, for the period 1800–1860, and the information for 1870 was calculated from Table XXVI, vol. II, U.S. Census, 1870.

16. As for the birth ratio equation, an indication of the explanatory power of the internal and total density variables can be provided by examining the R^2 resulting from an ordinary least-squares regression procedure, which, in this case, was equal to .73.

17. Of the 104 cases, all had residuals less than or equal to 15% of the actual values while 96% had residuals 10% or less of the actual values.

18. This equation assumes that in-migration and out-migration of children during the decade balances out. Since ultimately the number of children per one thousand people is estimated, the assumption of the fertility analysis is that children who enter a state as a proportion of the total amount of in-migration during a decade is equal to the number of children leaving as a proportion of the total amount of out-migration. The lack of migration data (even nativity information by state of current residence is unavailable before 1850) makes this assumption necessary in studies of this type.

19. This is consistent with a land availability model since land tended to be more easily available in the south.

20. Yasuba, *Birth Rates.*

21. This assumes that the adjustment factors that apply to the northern area also apply for the entire group of states and, therefore, they cancel out.

22. Since the proportion of reproductive females is assumed to have been the same in rural and urban areas (or, more realistically, that the rural proportion of reproductive females does not vary greatly from the total proportion of reproductive females since the percent of the population living in urban areas is quite small in most cases), the relationship between the rural birth ratio and the total birth ratio will be the sole factor used in the calculation of this adjustment factor.

23. Grabill, Kiser, and Whelpton, *Fertility,* provide information on a variant of the birth ratio: the number of children under 5 years of age per 1000 white women aged 20 to 44. They divided their data into regions and into

separate rural and urban components. Since almost all of the 23 states are either in the New England, Middle Atlantic, East North Central, or West North Central group (Delaware and Maryland are the two exceptions), a weighted average of the child-woman ratios for these regions can be calculated that roughly corresponds to the birth ratio for the northern area. This value can then be compared with the child-woman ratio for the entire United States. Similarly, the child-woman ratio for the rural areas of the regions containing most of the northern states can be compared with the total ratio for these regions. Finally, after assuming that the percentage difference between the number of white women aged 20 to 44 in the entire United States and the number contained within the smaller group of states was equal to the difference in the proportion of reproductive females calculated above, the same two decades can be analyzed. For the decade 1790–1800, the crude birth rate for all areas of all of the states was only 0.2% higher than the crude birth rate for rural areas of the northern states and, for the decade 1830–1840, it was 1.2% lower.

24. A number of fertility estimates have been made for the pre-1800 period. Grabill, Kiser, and Whelpton, *Fertility,* summarize the findings of both contemporary and modern researchers and place the crude birth rate during the Colonial and Early Federal periods within the 50–57 range. These values compare favorably with the 1790–1800 estimate of the fertility model which equaled 54.1. By the turn of the century, the estimated birth rate had fallen to about 53, above the birth rate of about 51 given by Lotka, "The Size of American Families," but within the range of 52–53 given by Blodget, *Economica.*

25. While there are little reliable data concerning crude birth rate estimates for specific states, some information of this type does exist. For example, Robert Gutman, "The Birth Statistics of Massachusetts During the Nineteenth Century," *Population Studies,* 10 (July 1956), 69–94, estimates the crude birth rate for the state of Massachusetts. Values for the mid-nineteenth century are: 35.1 for 1844–1846, 33.2 for 1849–1851, 33.2 for 1859–1861 and 28.4 for 1869–1871. These estimates apply to the white population in all areas of the state and, therefore, they must be adjusted to be comparable to the predictions of the fertility model. In 1840, the crude birth rate for rural Massachusetts was 8.5% greater than the crude birth rate for the entire state (using, again, the ratio of the rural birth ratio to the total birth ratio). Thus, the adjusted values of Gutman's estimates equal: 38.1 for 1844–1846, 36.0 for 1849–1851 and 1859–1861, and 30.8 for 1869–1871. The fertility model predicted a value of 37.0 for the decade lasting from 1840–1850, thereby lying within the range of the adjusted estimates. The prediction for the decade 1850–1860, 32.8, was slightly low when compared with Gutman's estimates, as was the prediction for the decade 1860–1870, 29.4. These differences are relatively small, however.

26. Meeker, "The Improving Health," and Yasuba, *Birth Rates.*

27. Meeker, "The Improving Health"; Robert Higgs, "Mortality in Rural America, 1870–1920: Estimates and Conjectures," *Explorations in Economic History,* 10 (Winter 1973), 177–195; and Simon Kuznets, "Long Swings in

Population Growth and Related Economic Variables," in Simon Kuznets, *Economic Growth and Structure, Selected Essays* (New York, 1965).

28. Vinovskis, "A Multivariate Regression," and Higgs, "Mortality."

29. Ansley J. Coale and Paul Demeny, *Regional Model Life Tables and Stable Populations* (Princeton, 1966).

30. Frederick Jackson Turner, "The Significance of the Frontier in American History," paper read at the meeting of the American Historical Association in Chicago, July 12, 1893. Reprinted in Turner, *The Frontier in American History* (New York, 1921), pp. 21–22.

31. It is presumed that the demand for children fell in older areas despite the availability of land in the West since there were considerable costs associated with setting up a viable farm in a relatively unsettled area (see Clarence H. Danhof, "Farm-Making Costs and the 'Safety-Valve': 1850–60," *Journal of Political Economy,* 49 (June 1941), 317–359). In addition, as mentioned previously, it is likely that parents preferred keeping the family residing within the same general vicinity.

32. Coale and Demeny, *Regional Model Life Tables.*

33. Coale and Zelnik, *New Estimates,* estimated that the enumeration error for native white males aged 0 to 9 in the 1880 census (the earliest census analyzed) was about 6.3% (the simple average of 9.1% for males aged 0 to 4 and 3.5% for males aged 5 to 9) while, for native white females, it was about 6.2% (the simple average of 9.1% for females aged 0 to 4 and 3.2% for females aged 5 to 9). Comparable figures for the 1890 census were 5.3% for males and 5.1% for females.

34. Grabill, Kiser, and Whelpton, *Fertility,* estimated an error of 6.2% for the native white population under 5 in the 1880 census. This estimate is low compared with Coale and Zelnik (about 9% for the native white population under age 5) and, since the enumeration error for children aged 5 to 9 is expected to be smaller than that of children aged 0 to 4, the total error for children aged 0 to 9 would probably be about 4 or 5 percent. In an examination of earlier censuses, they estimated enumeration errors for native white children aged 0 to 4 of 11.6%, 8.0% and 9.8% in 1870, 1860 and 1850. Given the relationship between under-enumeration of children aged 0 to 4 and those aged 5 to 9 (as found by Coale and Zelnik for the 1880 census), these estimates correspond roughly with enumeration errors for children aged 0 to 9 in the 5–8% range.

35. Coale and Zelnik, *New Estimates.*

Chapter IV

The Theory of Migration

> They [native Americans] are greater wanderers, less tied to home associations, than are the inhabitants of Europe. This fact is sufficiently accounted for by the vast extent of unoccupied land, and the great natural resources of the country, which have as yet hardly been touched.[1]

The above quotation attests to the fact that the magnitude of migration which had taken place within the United States during the nineteenth century had reached uncommon proportions. In this chapter, the factors which underlie the migration process will be identified and discussed within a theoretical framework. First, an overview of migration theory is presented (IV.1). Gravity-type models are discussed next (IV.2) and the selection of independent variables is considered (IV.3). Finally, conclusions are presented (IV.4). Later, in Chapter V, migration theory will be applied in estimating a migration model which will eventually serve as a key component in the settlement model presented in Chapter VI.

IV.1 GENERAL THEORETICAL BACKGROUND

It is not difficult to determine the starting point in the history of the study of migration. Ravenstein, in his two papers entitled "The Laws of Migration," developed a set of laws governing migration which he applied to the experience of a variety of countries, including the United States.[2] Briefly, these laws can be summarized as follows:

1. Migration is inversely related to distance;
2. Migration is a gradual process which is characterized by several stages or currents;
3. Each main current of migration produces a counter-current;
4. The rural propensity to migrate exceeds the urban propensity;
5. Technological change leads to an increase in migration over time;
6. The major factor in explaining migration streams is the economic motive.

Perhaps the most interesting aspect of Ravenstein's approach is his emphasis on the economic reasons underlying migration. Ravenstein concluded that the motivation for migration arose from the presence of geographic differentials in potential earnings which led to the movement of certain persons in an effort to increase their income:

> I do not question for a moment that the principal, though not the only cause of migration, has to be sought for in over-population in one part of the country, whilst there exist elsewhere underdeveloped resources which hold out greater promise for remunerative labor. . . . Bad or oppressive laws, heavy taxation . . . all have produced and are still producing currents of migration, but none of these currents can compare in volume with that which arises from the desire inherent in most men to 'better' themselves in material respects.[3]

Further, these general economic factors were of even greater importance in the case of the United States where, according to Ravenstein, there existed "exceptional wants" and "exceptional opportunities," leading to migration streams which covered relatively great distances.

Later work on U.S. migration similarly treated economic factors as important causal variables. Turner, for example, followed Ravenstein in believing that migration was the result of "economic" man's reaction to differences in earning opportunities.[4] Hicks also hypothesized that migration resulted from differences in economic advantage and, more recently, Lee developed a migration framework which went beyond Ravenstein's laws.[5] These early theorists contributed greatly to the development of what can be referred to as the current group of migration theories. Following the categorization presented by Sahota, this body of theory can be divided into three schools: human capital, selectivity, and push-pull.[6]

The first of these, the human capital approach, is associated with the "Chicago School." Here, the neoclassical theory of investment is applied to the migration decision and the costs and returns to migration are considered as the real value of expected net benefits is maximized. In other words, migration is treated as an act of investment whose purpose is to maximize the present value of the future earning stream net of costs. Thus, rational economic behavior is assumed and the migration decision is treated as a constrained utility maximization problem.

The selectivity approach is attributed mainly to Simon Kuznets and the "Harvard School." The major concern of this approach is not with the benefits and costs of migration but, rather, involves the composition of the migration stream. There are certain persons with high propensities to migrate and these persons are more likely to respond to differential earning prospects by migrating. The result of the migration of certain risk-takers is continued economic growth which, in turn, leads to further selective migration.

The final school of thought stems directly from Ravenstein and concentrates on the aspects of the area of origin which repel or push migrants and those aspects of the area of destination which attract or pull them. Specifically, both push and pull factors include all aspects of living conditions within the respective areas and, therefore, migration is treated as being a function of both economic and social differentials.

An examination of these "schools" shows that the distinction between them is more semantics than substance. The constrained utility maximization framework of the human capital approach considers the increase in net benefits associated with migration and, therefore, necessarily examines the expected net gain in utility associated with a move. Since the utility framework includes non-economic considerations, the calculation of the expected utility gain involves the relative attractiveness of the destination area and the costs of migrating and those factors are basically the same components used in the push-pull approach. Thus, the pull of a particular area can be represented by a vector of economic and non-economic characteristics which reflect the benefits associated with the destination area while a push vector can represent the benefits (or lack of benefits) of the area of origin. The difference is the expected utility gain and, if this exceeds the economic and non-economic costs of migrating, then migration would occur. In total, the push-pull approach fits into a more general human capital approach. A distinction arises in practice since the proponents of the human capital approach tend to stress economic considerations to the exclusion of non-economic factors while a typical push-pull study relies more on sociological factors, but there is no theoretical reason behind this difference.

The same is true for selectivity. As Sahota has pointed out, the "Chicago School" can "explain the migration of select people, for example, the younger, the better educated, or more enterprising people, by the expectancy of higher income differentials or longer payoff periods of the streams of future income, rather than merely saying that particular select groups have a higher propensity to migrate."[7] That the selectivity approach fits neatly within the human capital framework should come as no surprise since Kuznets has stated that: "internal migration and the redistribution of population by residence among various parts of the country are a major way in which people respond to changing economic opportunities emerging in the course of economic growth."[8] He goes on to explain that differential economic opportunities arise in different parts of the country and that changes in the geographic distribution of earnings and the costs of migration contribute to an increase in migration. While Kuznets concerns himself mainly with time-series changes in migration, his "school" is theoretically consistent with the others.

This is also the case with the two early migration theorists, Ravenstein and Turner. While Sahota places Ravenstein in the push-pull category, his concentration on the economic motive underlying migration seems to have more in common with the economic concern of the human capital school. He, along with Turner, treated migration as a response to geographic differences in economic opportunities and, therefore, their theories can be examined within the human capital framework of constrained utility maximization and rational economic behavior.

In total, the distinctions made with respect to migration theory do little more than indicate certain biases in approach. They do not seem to reflect actual theoretical differences since there exists an inner consistency within the various approaches. Thus, ignoring problems of semantics, the body of migration theory represents a coherent and related group of hypotheses which can be examined within a single theoretical framework.

IV.2 GRAVITY-TYPE MODELS

The dominant methodological approach in the study of internal migration involves the quantification of certain variables which are based on the theory of migration and the empirical analysis of these variables within a statistical model. The starting point for these models is the gravity model. Broadly speaking, a gravity model is simply an equation which measures the relationship between motion, mass and distance. Specifically, the flow between two areas is assumed to be positively related to the size of the origin and destination populations and inversely related to the distance between the two areas. A gravity model by itself is useless (at least in terms of the social sciences) unless its variables are taken to represent certain factors arising from theoretical considerations. A simple example of the adaptation of a gravity-type model to the explanation of migration was presented by Isard.[9] Isard took the first five of Ravenstein's laws and placed them within the context of an equation which measured the attraction between two areas as a function of population (P), distance (D), and additional factors (Z):

$$M_{ij} = P_i/D_{ij} \cdot f(Z_j) \qquad (1)$$

Here, the flow between points i and j (M_{ij}) is a positive function of the population of area i, an inverse function of the distance between the two points and, also, is a function of the attributes associated with area j (given by Z_j: a vector of characteristics). In this case, the basic gravity model has been modified and used to represent certain "laws" of migration. More generally, the gravity model can be expanded to include a large number of explanatory variables and used to explain a variety of economic phenomena.

Anderson presented what he referred to as a typical specification of the gravity equation:

$$M_{ijk} = a_k \cdot Y_i^{B1k} \cdot Y_j^{B2k} \cdot P_i^{B3k} \cdot P_j^{B4k} \cdot D_{ij}^{B5k} \cdot U_{ijk} \qquad (2)$$

where M_{ijk} represents the flow of factor k from area i to area j, Y_i and Y_j are incomes in i and j, P_i and P_j are populations in i and j, D_{ij} is the distance between the two areas and U_{ijk} is a log-normally distributed error term.[10] He developed a theoretical foundation for the use of this equation in the study of international and interregional commodity exchange and, thus, within this context, k refers to a particular commodity. However, k can represent people and M_{ijk} can measure gross migration between point i and point j. Of course, the use of a gravity-type model to explain migration flows involves the development of a theoretical framework similar to that developed by Anderson for the exchange of commodities. Since the general theory of migration has already been discussed, the next step in the formulation of a gravity-type model is to select a set of variables which can be fit into a broader version of Equation (2).

IV.3 SELECTION OF INDEPENDENT VARIABLES

The brief analysis of migration theory which was presented above centered on a number of different elements, all of which can be placed within two broad categories: benefits and costs. The calculation of the benefits associated with migration involves some measurement of the increase in utility and, therefore, is actually a relative term. Thus, characteristics of the area of origin must be considered along with those of the destination area. In this way, a utility differential can be calculated and the economic and social gains from migration can be compared with migration costs.

The availability of data typically dictates the selection of the particular variables which are used as proxies for the costs and benefits of migration. The ideal measure of economic benefits would be the increment to real earnings for individual m which is associated with their movement from area i to area j: $(E/P)_{j,m} - (E/P)_{i,m}$, where E is earnings and P is the price level. While the latter term may be calculated by examining measured income, the calculation of individual m's expected earnings in area j is a function of a number of personal characteristics including occupation, training, age, education, and other explanatory variables which affect income. In practice, the use of this sort of micro data is very rare and, instead, aggregate measures are used as proxies for regional differentials in earnings. For example, average real income by occupational group may be used or, as is more often the case, median per capita income may be used instead. Alternatively, the average real wage may be substituted for the income variable but, in either case, the difference between the value of the earnings variable in area j and the value in area i measures, in part, the benefits from migration.

There has been some controversy about the use of aggregate earnings variables in the calculation of benefits. It has been argued that the probability of employment is a more important determinant of migration than the level of wages or income. Specifically, the job opportunity thesis states that employment levels and employment growth should be used as proxies for economic benefits.[11] Therefore, differential employment measures are often included as independent variables in a migration equation along with wage and income variables.

Thus far, only economic benefits have been discussed. However, there are a wide range of variables which can be used as proxies for the non-economic elements in the utility function. For instance, people are more likely to migrate to an area which is relatively safe, has a favorable climate and offers certain recreational and cultural amenities. One variable which measures some of the non-economic determinants of migration is an urbanization variable. This variable is particularly important in a developing country where the city may offer the promise of a life-style which is preferred to that found in rural areas.[12] However, as is the case with most of the proxies for non-economic variables, there are problems of interpretation as it is often difficult to differentiate statistically between the lure of higher urban income and the attractiveness of other urban characteristics. A related variable with similar interpretive difficulties is some type of population density measure. While higher population density may encourage migration in the same manner as urbanization, population density may also indicate the extent of overcrowding which in rural areas, as was discussed above, may have repercussions in terms of potential earnings as well as having unfavorable non-economic effects.

The interpretation of education variables is also somewhat ambiguous. While the education of an individual is likely to be positively related to migration since a more educated person is better able to take advantage of opportunities which are available in a new area, the relationship between the average level of educational attainment within the origin and destination areas and the propensity to migrate is not clear. Higher levels of education in destination areas may indicate the presence of certain social amenities but, at the same time, may reflect greater competition for employment. Higher educational levels in the area of origin may imply the existence of favorable non-economic characteristics within the area, but also may mean that a greater percentage of the residents could benefit by migrating to a different area.

In total, the estimation of a gravity-type model which included the independent variables mentioned above would produce regression coefficients with signs that could not always be predicted beforehand. However, it is expected that higher real per capita income or average real wages, lower unemployment, and a greater extent of urbanization in the destination area and lower real per capita income or average real wages, higher unemployment, and a lesser degree of urbanization in the area of origin would all lead to a greater amount of migration between the two areas. The signs of the regression coefficients for origin and destination levels of education and of population density are indeterminate.

Proxies for the costs of migration must also be included in a gravity-type model since a positive benefits differential would lead to migration if and only if the gain in benefits offsets the costs of migrating. These costs can be separated into different components. The most obvious cost associated with migration is the direct cost of transportation. While this amount appears to be relatively small in most developed nations, this was not always the case, as illustrated by the nineteenth century United

States where transportation costs represented a non-trivial portion of family income. Yet, this may be the least important of the cost components. A second type of migration cost is non-economic. Uprooting from one area and settling in another involves adapting to new surroundings while leaving behind friends and family. Thus, a psychic cost of migration exists along with the monetary cost. Finally, there is the opportunity cost of migration resulting from the period of time during the move and immediately after arriving at the destination area when migrants are unemployed. As a result, there are foregone earnings which should be included in the calculation of the total migration cost.[13]

Usually, a single proxy for the cost of migration, the distance between the origin and destination areas, is included as an independent variable in the gravity-type model. The manner of measuring distance varies with the availability of data and the particular interest of the study. For example, the distance between two areas may be calculated in terms of railroad miles or, more simply, in terms of the number of miles between population centers. In any case, as the distance increases, the direct cost of transportation and the psychic cost increase. Thus, as Ravenstein pointed out in the first of his laws, migration is expected to be inversely related to distance. However, there is another determinant of migration which is related to distance but is not directly related to costs. There is a distinction between the expected real benefits of migration and the perceived benefits. Imperfect information means that some individuals who could maximize utility by migrating do not realize this and, therefore, do not migrate. Since uncertainty about conditions in a destination area increases with distance, the distance variable may measure the information flow as well as the psychic and monetary costs of migration.

In total, it is clear that the regression coefficient of the distance variable in a gravity-type model is expected to have a negative sign but it is not always clear what this variable actually represents. While it is likely that the relative importance of the different factors reflected in the distance variable varies with respect to the sample under consideration (in particular, with the development level of the area or nation), Schwartz has attempted to determine what underlies the success of the distance variable in explaining recent internal migration within the United States.[14] He examined the psychic cost and information level components of distance and tested to see which was of greater importance. First, he assumed that psychic costs increased with the age of the migrant while the information level increased with the education of the migrant. Then, he examined the absolute value of the distance elasticity for different age and educational groups and found out that the impact of the distance variable increased as the level of education decreased, while age had little effect on the regression coefficient of the distance variable. Thus, for the contemporary United States, it appears that the distance variable is a proxy for the level of information rather than for the psychic cost associated with migration.

The importance of the information level has been recognized in a number of studies and there have been attempts to measure this factor separately from the costs associated with the distance variable. One way which has met with some success is to include a measure of prior migration between two areas as an independent variable in explaining current migration. Presumably, the presence of a larger number of former inhabitants of area i residing within area j increases the level of the information flow between the areas, thereby decreasing the uncertainty faced by potential migrants in area i. However, this procedure can lead to the typical problems encountered when lagged dependent variables are included on the right-hand side of an equation. For example, the lagged variable may capture the previously unexplained variation and increase the explanatory power of the independent variables without representing any specific additional causal factors. Yet, if information is really that important in explaining migration (as indicated by Schwartz's analysis), then including lagged migration as an independent variable can be defended on theoretical grounds.

Now that a group of independent variables has been selected, all of which arise from the general theory of migration, the theoretical foundation for different formulations of the gravity-type model can be discussed. While Anderson showed how a basic gravity-type model (Equation (2)) is consistent with the theory of commodity exchange, it can also be shown how the same explanatory variables can be examined within a migration framework. The income variables can be directly interpreted with the income in the destination area, Y_j, and the income in the area of origin, Y_i, representing the differential earning opportunities associated with migration between the two areas and the signs of the regression coefficients are expected to be positive and negative, respectively.[15]

The role of the population variables is less obvious than that of the income variables. The population of the destination area, P_j, may reflect the opportunity for employment and, thus, would be expected to be positively related to migration. However, a larger population may also indicate overcrowding which would inhibit migration, especially in rural areas where a large population may imply a scarcity of available farmland. On the other hand, if the population of the area of origin, P_i, were to reflect the availability of land then it would be positively associated with migration. Moreover, if the dependent variable represented the number of migrants rather than the percentage of those migrating who go to a particular destination, then this would also lead to a positive sign for the regression coefficient of the origin population since the larger the population, the greater are the chances that there would be a group of people who are motivated to migrate. Finally, the distance variable, D_{ij}, is expected to be inversely related to migration regardless of whether this variable reflects the direct cost of transportation, the psychic cost of migration or the level of information. Thus, each of the variables in Equation (2) have been evaluated in terms of migration theory and there exists a theoretical rationale for using this equation in a migration analysis. The same is true with other, more complete gravity-type models.

IV.4 CONCLUSION

There are a large number of studies which use gravity-type models to help explain migration patterns.[16] The particular specification of these models reflects the bias in approach with some studies centering on certain push or pull characteristics, some dealing mainly with the question of selectivity by analyzing the composition of the migration stream and others relying on a stricter application of the human capital approach. The theoretical framework discussed above will be used in specifying and estimating a gravity-type model which will later be part of the settlement model.

NOTES AND REFERENCES

1. E. G. Ravenstein, "The Laws of Migration," *Journal of the Royal Statistical Society,* LII (June 1889), 241–301 (quote from pp. 280–281). Also in Reprint No. S-483 of the "Bobbs-Merrill Series in the Social Sciences."
2. E. G. Ravenstein, "The Laws," (June 1889) and "The Laws of Migration," *Journal of the Royal Statistical Society,* XLVIII (June 1885), 167–227. Also in Reprint No. S-482 of the "Bobbs-Merrill Series in the Social Sciences."
3. Ravenstein, "The Laws," (June 1889), p. 286.
4. Turner, "The Significance." See his quotation cited earlier in section III.4.
5. J. R. Hicks, *The Theory of Wages* (New York, 1932) and Everett S. Lee, "A Theory of Migration," *Demography,* 3 (No. 1, 1966).
6. Gian S. Sahota, "An Economic Analysis of Internal Migration in Brazil," *Journal of Political Economy,* 76 (March/April 1968), 218–245.
7. Sahota, "An Economic Analysis," p. 220.
8. Simon Kuznets, "Introduction: Population Redistribution, Migration, and Economic Growth," in *Population Redistribution, and Economic Growth, U.S., 1870–1950,* Vol. 3, H. T. Eldridge and D. S. Thomas, eds. (Philadelphia, 1964), p. xxiii.
9. Walter Isard, *Methods of Regional Analysis: An Introduction to Regional Science* (Cambridge, 1960). This is referred to as a gravity-type model rather than a gravity model since it includes variables other than population and distance and, in addition, the latter two variables are given theoretical content.
10. James E. Anderson, "A Theoretical Foundation for the Gravity Equation," *American Economic Review,* 69 (March 1979), 106–116.
11. The job opportunity thesis is also referred to as the job vacancies thesis. See Herbert S. Parnes, *Research on Labor Mobility: An Appraisal of Research Findings in the United States,* Social Science Research Bulletin 65, 1954.
12. Even though, of course, the promise may not be realized.
13. When the benefit measure is earnings in the destination area rather than differential earnings, all income which would have been earned had migration not occurred should be considered as part of the opportunity cost of migration.
14. Aba Schwartz, "Interpreting the Effect of Distance on Migration," *Journal of Political Economy,* 81 (Sept./Oct. 1973), 1153–1169.
15. This specification would be subject to estimation problems unless the values of the income variables are taken at some time prior to when the migration variable was calculated since income levels in the two areas are functions of migration and, therefore, simultaneous equations bias would affect the estimated coefficients.

16. For examples of studies dealing with developing countries see Sahota, "An Economic Analysis"; Michael J. Greenwood, "The Determinants of Labor Migration in Egypt," *Journal of Regional Science,* 9 (August 1969), 283–290; Manuel J. Carvajal and David T. Geithman, "An Economic Analysis of Migration in Costa Rica," *Economic Development and Cultural Change,* 23 (Oct. 1974), 105–122; Evangelos M. Falaris, "The Determinants of Internal Migration in Peru: An Economic Analysis," *Economic Development and Cultural Change,* 27 (Jan. 1979), 327–341; John M. Munro, "Migration in Turkey," *Economic Development and Cultural Change,* 22 (July 1974), 634–653; and T. Paul Schultz, "Rural-Urban Migration in Colombia," *The Review of Economics and Statistics,* 53 (May 1971), 157–163. Most of the work dealing with internal migration in the United States concerns the post-World War II period (this is particularly true for studies using gravity-type models). See, for example, L. E. Gallaway, R. F. Gilbert and P. E. Smith, "The Economics of Labor Mobility: An Empirical Analysis," *Western Economic Journal,* V (June 1967), 211–223; Michael J. Greenwood, "An Analysis of the Determinants of Geographic Labor Mobility in the United States," *The Review of Economics and Statistics,* 51 (May 1969), 189–194; and Edward Miller, "Is Out-Migration Affected by Economic Conditions?" *Southern Economic Journal,* 39 (Jan. 1973), 396–405. An interesting study of a slightly earlier period was done by C. Horace Hamilton, "Population Pressure and Other Factors Affecting Net Rural-Urban Migration," *Social Forces,* 30 (Dec. 1951), 209–215. Finally, for a comprehensive examination of internal migration in the United States during several periods of history (ranging from the early 1800s to the present) see Lowell E. Gallaway and Richard K. Vedder, "Mobility of Native Americans," *Journal of Economic History,* XXXI (Sept. 1971), 613–649. This study will be discussed in Chapter V.

Chapter V

An Internal Migration Model

The analysis presented in the preceding chapter will now be applied in producing a gravity-type model for the historical United States. Although a variety of measures and techniques will be tested, life-time data, a gross measure for the dependent variable, and independent variables which are based on theory consistent with the human capital framework are eventually employed. After background and methodological issues are discussed (V.1), the gravity-type model is specified (V.2) and estimated (V.3). Finally, conclusions are presented (V.4).

V.1 BACKGROUND AND METHODOLOGICAL ISSUES

The study of internal migration in the United States does not involve a single migration stream but, rather, includes four separate currents: east to west, south to north, rural to urban, and urban to suburban.[1] While rural-urban and south-north migration will be considered in Chapter VI (urban-suburban migration was largely a twentieth century phenomenon and is not relevant here), the east-west movement of the population will be of primary interest. In fact, the movement of the population from the eastern to the western regions of the United States during the course of the nineteenth century is one of the most dramatic aspects of U.S. development. Indeed, Turner claimed in his seminal paper of 1893 that, "The existence of an area of free land, its continuous recession, and the advance of

American settlement westward, explain American development."[2]

There are a number of possible ways to measure and to analyze migration. In terms of the migration variable, the two choices involve the use of gross and net rates. The former considers the total number of persons migrating from point i to point j, while the latter measures the difference between the number going from point i to point j and the number going from point j to point i. Thus, the net rate between points i and j is the difference between the gross rate from point i and the gross rate from point j. It is generally agreed, however, that the preferred migration variable is a gross measure.[3] Therefore, in an effort to utilize the available information in the most efficient manner possible, this analysis will center on gross migration.

There are also choices to be made concerning the nature of the data.[4] Briefly, information on migration can be computed from several types of sources. For example, data can be supplied directly from surveys, population registers or censuses or, alternatively, data can be calculated indirectly through the use of a residual method. Further, the migration measure may be short-term, reflecting migration which had occurred within a given period of time (for example, within the preceding five years), or, instead, it may be life-time. The latter case is typically found when census data are used to determine the migration pattern at a particular time and there is no prior information which can be used to determine the stream of migration between two specific dates.

The earliest U.S. information on the distribution of the migration flow among states is found in the 1850 census which presents nativity data by state of present residence. Thus, the migration data at this date are life-time and are subject to the advantages and disadvantages corresponding to data of this type. On the negative side, intermediate migration is ignored as migration from state i to state j_1 which is followed by migration from state j_1 to state j_2 would only be counted as migration between states i and j_2 if the migrant were residing in state j_2 at the time of the census. In addition, there is no fixed time period in which migration had taken place since people living in state j at the census date who were born in state i had migrated over an indefinite period of time. However, this indeterminacy may be an advantage in terms of the study of the historical United States. As Gallaway and Vedder pointed out, the lifetime data given in the 1850 census reflect migration over most of the history of the United States since some of the migration had occurred during the beginning of the nineteenth century and even earlier.[5] In sum, data from the 1850 census may be used to compute a dependent variable for use in a gravity-type model, $M_{ij,t_1 \rightarrow 1850}$, which measures migration from state i to stage j during the period ending in the year 1850.

Alternatively, since the censuses after 1850 include nativity data, the change in the number of people living in state j who were born in state i over the dates at which the two censuses were taken may be computed. For example, $M_{ij,t_1 \rightarrow 1860} - M_{ij,t_1 \rightarrow 1850}$ can be used to provide an estimate of migration from state i to state j during the decade lasting from 1850 to 1860.[6] There are several advantages to this approach. For one, the possibility of intermediate migration is smaller due to the shorter time period under examination and, in addition, the migration measure represents a decade rate which is the same time unit which had been used in the fertility model.

In total, the list of dependent variables will include gross migration measures for the period ending in 1850 and for each of the decades 1850 to 1860, 1860 to 1870, 1870 to 1880 and 1880 to 1890.[7] The ultimate selection of a dependent variable will be made on empirical grounds after the rest of the gravity model has been specified and then estimated.

V.2 SPECIFICATION OF THE MODEL

While the selection of the dependent variable involves a range of possibilities and is subject to discussion, the set of independent variables stems directly from the theory of migration. The basic assumption of the most general approach, human capital, is that individuals make investment decisions with the aim of maximizing utility. Thus, migration would be induced by the presence of positive net benefits associated with a move between two areas. Both benefits and costs may be psychic or monetary and, as was detailed in Chapter IV, certain independent variables are typically used as proxies for these elements. In the case of differential economic benefits, it is common that income or wage variables for the destination and origin regions are used while a distance variable normally measures migration costs. For the gravity-type model which will be estimated here, these types of variables will be used but, given the peculiarities of U.S. historical data and the focus of this study, some modifications will be made.

The first area to be discussed involves the gains to migration. This analysis centers on rural migration and, therefore, some measure of the differences between rural earning prospects in the destination area and rural income in the area of origin is needed. Historical data on per capita income by state, when available, fail to differentiate between the urban and rural components of income, and in states which have a relatively large degree of urbanization, this variable is likely to be a poor indicator of rural income. On the other hand, there is a variable which is determined solely by rural conditions and, therefore, may be used to represent both the current level of rural income and the prospective level. This variable had been an integral part of the fertility model and its use here would be highly desirable for practical as well as theoretical reasons. The variable in question is a measure of the availability of land and has been referred to as the internal density measure.[8] As discussed above, a large value of the internal density measure would mean that land was difficult to acquire and, moreover, that earning prospects were poor.

It seems reasonable to assume that the rural population, who during this period of time relied heavily on agriculture as their primary source of income, would have calculated the economic benefits of a state in terms of rural population density and the availability of land. This had been the feeling of Gallaway and Vedder who, in explaining internal migration in the nineteenth century United States, had included a land availability variable in their gravity-type model.[9] They too used a population density measure as a proxy for the ease of acquiring new land and this variable proved to be an important factor in explaining interstate migration.

Whether the land availability variable is simply a proxy for prospective earnings or it represents a more involved notion such as the ability to provide for some predetermined level of the intergenerational transfer of wealth (along the lines of the bequest theory discussed in Chapter II), this variable serves as a proxy for the benefits of migration. Therefore, a potential migrant would prefer a state with a large amount of available land (indicated by a small value of the internal density variable) to a state where available land was scarce. Further, out-migration would be encouraged when the amount of available land in a prospective destination state exceeded the amount in the state of origin while the opposite would have a dampening effect. Thus, a measure of differential land availability could serve as a proxy for differential economic benefits.

In total, it is expected that migration between any two states would depend, at least in part, on the differences in the availability of land between the states. Therefore, the first independent variable is the difference between the internal density measure of the state of origin i and the internal density measure of the destination state j, both at a given time t:

$$IR_{i,t} - IR_{j,t}. \tag{1}$$

The maximum value of this difference is one when the rural areas of state i are completely settled and the rural areas of state j are totally empty and the minimum value is negative one when the reverse is true. While this variable is symmetrical with respect to zero, there is no reason to expect that the relationship between the difference and the migration variable would be linear. Instead, it seems likely that a nonlinear relationship would be present. This would result if migration decreased with the decline in the difference in population densities until the state of origin was less densely settled than the destination state (implying that the availability difference variable had a negative value), at which point the benefits of migration would be zero and out-migration from state i to state j would be expected to cease. After the entire gravity-type model has been specified, the exact form of the relationship between the difference in land availability and the migration measure will be tested empirically.

Now that a measure of the economic gain from migration has been computed, proxies for the costs of migration can be discussed. Clearly, the existence of a positive benefits value is not sufficient to insure migration since the costs of migrating may outweigh the benefits. Thus, it is important to derive adequate measures for migration costs. As described in the survey of the migration literature, the costs of migrating between an origin state i and a destination state j are usually represented by a distance variable, D_{ij}. This variable is typically computed by taking the number of miles between population centers and this method will be applied in this study.[10]

As discussed above, the distance variable serves as a proxy for several types of migration costs. The direct cost of transportation is a positive function of distance as is the psychic cost. In addition, the distance variable measures the extent of the information flow since, given imperfect information, there is a distinction between expected real benefits and perceived benefits. This results in a miscalculation of the gains to migration for some prospective migrants and their failure to migrate despite the fact that, if they had, they would have been maximizing utility. Since uncertainty about conditions within a potential destination area is greater as the distance between it and the area of origin increases, the distance variable represents the level of information along with the pecuniary and nonpecuniary costs of migration. Regardless of whether the distance variable reflects information, transportation costs or psychic costs, it is expected that distance and migration are inversely related and, therefore, the coefficient of the distance variable in the gravity-type model should be negative.

Despite the common use of a distance variable as a proxy for the costs of migration, it is a rather crude measure. A given number of miles is assumed to have the same inhibiting effect on migration regardless of similarities and differences between the origin and destination areas. For example, the distance between population centers in Nebraska and Iowa is about 300 miles while the distance between Nebraska and South Dakota is only about 200 miles. Yet, since the characteristics of Iowa are more similar to Nebraska than are the characteristics of South Dakota, the psychic and economic costs associated with migration between Nebraska and South Dakota are likely to be higher than those resulting from migration between Nebraska and Iowa. Thus, the distance variable, in only measuring geographical distances, ignores other important determinants of migration costs.

Gallaway and Vedder, in an attempt to distinguish between differing costs of distance arising from aspects of the origin and destination states, included a regional affinity variable as an independent variable along with the distance variable.[11] In their study, a distance of m miles would be a far more powerful deterrent to migration if it meant leaving one region and going to another than if both states were in the same region. Thus, the desire to remain within an area with the same general characteristics as the origin is measured, but since Gallaway and Vedder divide the United States into only four large regions this variable is still rather crude. Similarly, regional dummy variables, used in several of the gravity-type models dealing with internal migration in a number of less developed countries throughout the world, reflect the same type of reasoning and are also crude measures of the affinity between regions.

In sum, regional affinity variables are often used since it is assumed that individuals desire to remain in an area with the same type of characteristics. In an analysis of the historical rural population, this can be translated roughly into the desire to continue with the same type of farming activities. While the group of states under examination was chosen in an effort to minimize the heterogeneity of the economic and social structure of the entire area, there are important differences remaining between the states. Many of these differences result from variations in climate and terrain which account for the basic pattern of agricultural activity. These differences tend to correspond with the latitudinal location of the states since areas which are an equal distance from the equator are more likely to have a similar climate and, to a lesser extent, similar terrain.[12] Thus, latitudinal deviations in either direction (north or south), in general reduce the affinity between regions, thereby increasing the costs of migration.

A regional affinity variable which is based on differences in latitude can be used to modify the distance variable while representing an improvement on the variables used by Gallaway and Vedder and the others. The magnitude of the north-south deviation between a destination state j and an origin state i, N-

S_{ij}, can be calculated by taking the difference between the latitudes of the two states:

$$N\text{-}S_{ij} = |LAT_j - LAT_i| \qquad (2)$$

Since $N\text{-}S_{ij}$ is based on the desire to remain at the same latitude, the direction of the vertical movement is irrelevant and, for this reason, the absolute value of the latitudinal difference is the pertinent measure. Larger values of the regional affinity variable imply greater psychic and economic costs of migration and, therefore, this variable is expected to be inversely related to migration.

Returning to the example given above, this new variable modifies the effect of the distance variable. Since the distance between Nebraska and South Dakota is 200 miles and the distance between Nebraska and Iowa is 300 miles, a negative regression coefficient for the distance variable would indicate that the gravity-type model would predict that the migration flow from Nebraska to South Dakota would exceed the flow from Nebraska to Iowa, all else being equal. However, the regional affinity variable has a value of 2 in the former case and 1 in the latter. A negative regression coefficient for this variable would indicate that there would be a greater volume of migration between Nebraska and Iowa than between Nebraska and South Dakota, thereby at least partially offsetting the effect of the distance variable. The smaller value of $N\text{-}S_{ij}$ for Nebraska and Iowa reflects the similar climate and terrain between these two states and the resulting fact that, for the most part, the states rely on a common agricultural activity (the growing of corn). In this example, if the regional affinity variable had been omitted (or, possibly, even if a regional dummy system had been employed), then the crudity of the distance variable would have led to inaccurate forecasts of interstate migration. Thus, at least in theory, this variable is an important refinement of the distance variable since it serves as a proxy for many of the costs of migration which are ignored in the total distance value given by D_{ij}.[13] Together, these variables can serve as proxies for migration costs, both on an aggregate level through the distance variable and on a more fine-tuned level through the regional affinity variable.

There is another directional consideration which the distance variable ignores besides the north-south movement represented by the regional affinity variable. While people are likely to prefer to remain at roughly the same latitude and, therefore, would desire to migrate in a horizontal rather than a vertical direction, a particular lateral direction is favored. For a variety of reasons, westward migration appears to have been more desirable than migration eastward. This may have resulted from non-economic factors such as the desire to start a new life and to settle a new area or may have involved economic factors concerning future earnings. It is reasonable to expect that as an area is settled, the more fertile land is the first to be cultivated. Eventually, when an area reaches advanced levels of settlement, only marginal land remains available. Thus, available land in the relatively developed east would be of poorer quality than available land in the west since this land has been passed over during the westward expansion. For this reason, if land were available in the east and in the west, land in the west would be preferred since it is likely that it would be of higher quality and, therefore, it would hold the promise of higher earnings in the future.

The formulation of an east-west directional variable differs from the previous one. In the case of the regional affinity variable, an increased vertical deviation reduced the migration flow. Here, the magnitude of the east-west difference is not of interest, only the direction. Thus, the east-west variable, $E\text{-}W_{ij}$, is calculated in two parts. First, the difference between the longitude of the destination state j and the longitude of the state of origin i is computed:

$$LGD_{ij} = LONG_j - LONG_i. \tag{3}$$

Then, if this difference is positive, the east-west variable takes on a value of one and, if not, it takes on a value of zero:

$$E\text{-}W_{ij} = \begin{matrix} 1 \text{ if } LGD_{ij} > 0 \\ 0 \text{ if } LGD_{ij} \leq 0 \end{matrix} \tag{4}$$

Therefore, the east-west variable is a dummy variable with a value of one when migration is to the west and with a value of zero when migration is to the east. If, in reality, westward migration were favored, then the regression coefficient of this variable would be positive.

Thus far, the list of independent variables includes a proxy for the benefits of migration ($IR_{i,t} - IR_{j,t}$), proxies for the cost of migration (D_{ij} and $N\text{-}S_{ij}$), and a variable which measures both benefits and tastes ($E\text{-}W_{ij}$). These variables are consistent with the human capital approach and are modified versions of the explanatory variables suggested in Chapter IV. There is one more variable which should be included and it reflects the specification of the dependent variable and the method of incorporating the data in the regression procedure.

The main dependent variable in this analysis is a measure of gross migration between the origin state i and the destination state j. This variable represents the total number of migrants rather than the percentage of those leaving state i who migrate to state j. Thus, the gravity-type model is in absolute rather than relative terms. If the regression procedure were carried out separately for each of the origin states, then the total number of out-migrants leaving state i would be irrelevant but, if the states were pooled, then the number leaving any given origin state i who go to a destination state j would depend, in part, on the magnitude of the out-migration flow from state i. Therefore, when all of the states are examined together, a measure of rural out-migration, $ROM_{s=i,t_1 \rightarrow t_2}$ must be included as an independent variable in the gravity-type model since it represents a scale factor which places the model in relative terms unaffected by absolute amounts.[14]

V.3 ESTIMATION RESULTS

The specification of the gravity-type model has now been completed. This model, with its variables as defined above, is as follows:

$$M_{ij,t_1 \rightarrow t_2} = f(IR_{i,t_3} - IR_{j,t_3}, D_{ij}, N\text{-}S_{ij}, E\text{-}W_{ij}, ROM_{s=i,t_1 \rightarrow t_2}, r) \quad (5)$$

where r is the error term. As discussed above, there are several possible dates for t_1 and t_2 and, given these values, the date of the availability difference variable (t_3) may be determined. For instance, if short-term migration data were used from the decade lasting from 1850 to 1860, t_3 would be equal to 1850 since it is presumed that the availability of land at the beginning of the decade determines migration during the decade.

The results from using the short-term gross migration data were poor, not only when each of the states of origin were examined separately but also when the entire sample was included in a single regression equation. In general, the explanatory power of the independent variables deteriorated over time with the data from the decade starting in 1850 producing results, which, while being the best produced by the short-term data, were nonetheless unacceptable.[15] This was also true when net migration rates were substituted for the gross rates.

The earlier data produced vastly superior results. These data, found in the 1850 census, are life-time data and reflect prior migration which had occurred during the first half of the nineteenth century and before. The indeterminancy of the starting point for migration raises questions about the proper date of the availability difference variable; therefore, alternative dates were tested. The statistical results indicated that the 1830 value of this variable worked best in explaining 1850 life-time migration. A twenty-year lag seems reasonable since a substantial portion of the total number of migrants probably migrated sometime between 1830 and 1850. Further, the presence of this lag reduces the problems of simultaneous equations bias found in studies where the independent variables are computed for a time which corresponds directly with the period of migration.

The two alternative methods of compiling the data for use in the regression procedure produced somewhat different results. When each state of origin was examined independently, the independent variables were only moderately successful in explaining the choice of destination state. This was likely due to the small number of degrees of freedom. As had been found by Gallaway, Gilbert and Smith in their analysis of a later period, when a pooled set of data was used, the results improved substantially.[16]

Both gross and net migration measures were used and, as expected, the measure of gross migration worked best. An or-

Table V.1. The Gravity-Type Model: Regression Results

Dependent Variable	*Constant*	$IR_{i,1830}$-$IR_{j,1830}$	D_{ij}	$N\text{-}S_{ij}$	$E\text{-}W_{ij}$	$ROM_{s=i,t_1 \rightarrow 1850}$
$LN(M_{ij,t_1 \rightarrow 1850})$	7.861	1.972	−.282	−.335	1.020	.005
	(31.5)[a]	(7.6)[a]	(10.7)[a]	(7.2)[a]	(4.0)[a]	(7.9)[a]
R^2 = .700	F Value = 140.2[a]					

Note: Absolute values of t-statistics are in parentheses.
[a]Significant at the 99% level.

dinary least-squares regression procedure was carried out several times in testing for the functional form of the gravity-type model. The best results were associated with an exponential specification (leading to an inverse semi-logarithmic estimation equation) reflecting the expected nonlinearity in the relationship between migration and the availability difference and distance variables. The estimated equation, with the dependent variable being the logarithm of the gross life-time migration variable, is presented in Table V.1.[17]

The results from the estimation of the gravity-type model are consistent with the theory of migration. Each independent variable has the expected sign and is significant at the highest conventional test levels. As the amount of available land in the destination state j increases relative to the amount in the state of origin i (implying a larger value of the availability difference variable), migration from state i to state j increases while migration decreases as the distance between the states grows. Further, migration decreases as the regional affinity between the two states becomes smaller, as indicated by a larger absolute value of the latitudinal deviation variable. Finally, the number of migrants going from state i to state j increases when the destination state is west of the state of origin and when the total number of out-migrants from state i increases. In total, each of the independent variables explains some portion of the cross-sectional variation in destination choice and together have accounted for 70% of the total variation.

V.4 CONCLUSION

A gravity-type model has been estimated which works reasonably well in explaining the pattern of internal migration during the first half of the nineteenth century. Once again, it should be noted, land availability played a prominent role in the analysis as a differential land availability measure proved to be an important explanatory variable helping to explain the selection of destination states by out-migrants. Thus, as land became increasingly scarce within a state, not only did birth rates fall but the attractiveness of the state as a potential destination also declined. For highly settled states, the combination of a low rate of natural increase and little in-migration led to a low rate of population growth. For states with a great deal of available land, high birth rates led to a high rate of natural increase which, along with a large amount of in-migration, resulted in rapid population growth. The relationship between the availability of land, net migration, and fertility rates is examined in detail in Chapter VI.

NOTES AND REFERENCES

1. See Conrad Taeuber and Irene B. Taeuber, *The Changing Population of the United States* (New York, 1958).
2. Turner, "The Significance," p. 1.
3. See Miller, "Is Out-Migration Affected," p. 396, and Larry A. Sjaastad, "The Costs and Returns of Human Migration," *Journal of Political Economy*, 70 (Oct. 1962), 80–93.
4. For a detailed analysis of a variety of data issues see Isard, *Methods of Regional Analysis;* P. H. Rees, "The Measurement of Migration, From Census Data and Other Sources," *Environment and Planning*, 9 (A 1977), 247–272; and Everett S. Lee, Ann Ratner Miller, Carol P. Brainard and Richard A. Easterlin, *Population Redistribution and Economic Growth, U.S., 1870–1950, Vol. 1, Methodological Considerations* (Philadelphia, 1957).
5. Gallaway and Vedder, "Mobility."
6. Due to the effects of mortality, this is a lower estimate of gross interstate migration.
7. As pointed out below, net migration measures were also tested but, as expected, the statistical results were inferior.
8. See Table I.2. As will be explained in Chapter VI, using this density measure as an explanatory variable in the gravity-type equation allows the key causal relationships in the settlement model to be endogenous.
9. Gallaway and Vedder, "Mobility."
10. Since the center of population of each state changes over time, the value of the distance variable between any two states will be an estimate of the average distance between population centers.
11. Gallaway and Vedder, "Mobility."
12. Richard H. Steckel, "The Economic Foundations of East-West Migration during the 19th Century," *Explorations in Economic History*, 20 (1983), 14–36, explains why U.S. migrants tended to minimize vertical movements in terms of seeds that were adapted to a given latitude and to the latitude-specific skills of farmers.
13. Yet, this regional affinity variable is far from being perfect. It is still a rather crude measure of regional similarities with respect to agricultural activity. Ideally, such features as the length of the growing season and the type of terrain would be specifically measured, but, for the purposes of the present study, it was felt that the affinity variable calculated above would suffice.
14. Gallaway and Vedder, "Mobility," examine each state separately

rather than pool their observations across states. In the later case, migration between each origin state i and each destination state j is considered in a single equation with i × j observations. In the former case, a single origin state i is examined in each regression with only j observations in the sample set. Each of these methods is tested below. When each state of origin is examined separately, the scale variable is excluded from the list of independent variables and, in addition, all of the characteristics of the state of origin i are ignored since they are the same for each of the observations in the sample. Thus, the internal density value for state i is eliminated as the economic benefits of migration are represented solely by the internal density measure for the destination state j.

15. It is not unexpected that this particular gravity-type model would have difficulty in explaining the pattern of U.S. internal migration after mid-century. It is important to recognize that the selection of independent variables was made with the purpose of analyzing rural migration and that variables such as the degree of urbanization and the level of urban income were omitted. Yet, the migration data do not differentiate between rural and urban migration and, during the latter part of the nineteenth century, urbanization became increasingly important in the United States. For this reason, migration data recorded during the second half of the century are of limited use in a study concerned with explaining demographic changes in rural areas. In Chapter VI, when the gravity-type equation is incorporated into the settlement model, it will be used to allocate out-migrants from rural areas to other rural areas while urban in-migration is treated separately. Thus, the use of migration data which fail to distinguish between rural and urban areas should not interfere with the ultimate purpose of the gravity-type model.

16. Gallaway, Gilbert and Smith, "The Economics."

17. While the dependent variable is identical to that used by Gallaway and Vedder, "Mobility," the independent variables are not. They used state data on population density in 1850, per capita income in 1840, wealth in 1860, and the number of employed free males in 1850 to capture the benefits of migration. For costs, they used the distance between major population centers in various states and a regional affinity dummy variable representing four broad areas of the country (northern, temperate, southern humid, and southern dry). While Gallaway and Vedder refer to their population density variable as a proxy for land availability this is not necessarily the case. A state may have a good deal of available land in rural sections but the presence of a large city would increase population density, thereby incorrectly indicating a lack of available farmland. $IR_{i,1830} - IR_{j,1830}$ measures the rural population exclusively and avoids the problem of confusing urbanization with low land availability. Further, causal variables explaining migration before 1850 should be lagged accordingly. With the exception of per capita income, the variables used by Gallaway and Vedder were not lagged and, in the case of wealth, the data postdated 1850.

Chapter VI

A Settlement Model

The principal purpose of this chapter is to specify a settlement model which replicates U.S. population growth and distribution and to use it to identify those factors which contributed to the settlement of the rural north during the period in which the greatest part of the settlement process occurred, 1790 to 1900.[1] First the settlement model is presented (VI.1) and then it is used to replicate the actual U.S. experience (VI.2). Alternative scenarios are examined next (VI.3) and conclusions are presented (VI.4). Finally, some additional tables containing supplementary state-specific predictions are presented in an appendix (VI.5).

VI.1 THE MODEL

In earlier chapters, fertility and migration models have been produced using partial equilibrium analyses in which the explanatory variables were treated as exogenously determined. These models are now combined to produce a single settlement model in which the key independent variables are endogenous, the interaction between the different demographic models can be examined, and feedbacks (for example, from higher out-migration to changes in fertility and back to migration) can be traced. Once again, density variables reflecting the growth and distribution of the rural population are computed and these are the key predictions of the settlement model which are used to evaluate its success in reproducing the course of U.S. demographic history.

The complete settlement model is as follows:

$$(1000C/W)_{s,t+10} = 2268.03 - 978.44(IR_{s,t}) - 819.15(TR_t) \quad (1)$$

$$(1000W/P)_{s,t+10} = 180.12 + 29.21(IR_{s,t}) + 49.14(TR_t) \quad (2)$$

$$CBR_{s,t\to t+10} = (1000C/W)_{s,t+10} \cdot (1000W/P)_{s,t+10} \cdot .000153 \quad (3)$$

$$RNI_{s,t\to t+10} = (CBR_{s,t\to t+10} - 22)/100 \quad (4)$$

$$OM_{s,t\to t+10} = \begin{cases} RP_{s,t}(RNI_{s,t\to t+10} + 1) + EIM_{s,t\to t+10}(RNI_{s,t\to t+10}/2 + 1) - MRP_s & \text{if } EX_{s,t} > 0 \\ 0 & \text{if } EX_{s,t} \le 0 \end{cases} \quad (5)$$

$$ROM_{s,t\to t+10} = \%R_t \cdot OM_{s,t\to t+10} \quad (6)$$

$$s = \begin{cases} j \text{ if } OM_{s,t\to t+10} = 0 \\ i \text{ if } OM_{s,t\to t+10} > 0 \end{cases} \quad (7)$$

$$M_{ij,t\to t+10} = e^{(7.8608 + 1.9718(IR_{i,t} - IR_{j,t}) - .2821(D_{ij}) - .3345(N\text{-}S_{ij}) + 1.0202(E\text{-}W_{ij}) + .005(ROM_{s=i,t\to t+10}))} \quad (8)$$

$$AM_{ij,t\to t+10} = M_{ij,t\to t+10} \cdot (ROM_{s=i,t\to t+10}/\Sigma_j M_{ij,t\to t+10}) \quad (9)$$

$$RIM_{s,t\to t+10} = \begin{cases} \Sigma_i AM_{ij,t\to t+10} & \text{if } s = j \\ 0 & \text{if } s = i \end{cases} \quad (10)$$

$$RP_{s,t+10} = RP_{s,t}(RNI_{s,t\to t+10} + 1) + EIM_{s,t\to t+10}(RNI_{s,t\to t+10}/2 + 1) + RIM_{s,t\to t+10} - OM_{s,t\to t+10} \quad (11)^a$$

[a]If adding $RIM_{s,t\to t+10}$ to $(RP_{s,t}(RNI_{s,t\to t+10}+1) + EIM_{s,t\to t+10}(RNI_{s,t\to t+10}/2 + 1))$ produces a total which exceeds MRP_s, then state s switches classification from j to i and the excess is re-

distributed among rural areas of the states which have retained their j classifications.

where

s	signifies state s
t	signifies time t
RP	is the rural population
MRP	is the maximum rural population
C	is the number of children aged 0 to 9
W	is the number of women aged 16 to 44
P	is the population
IR	is the internal density ratio; the ratio of the rural population of a particular state to its maximum rural population
TR	is the total density ratio; the ratio of the total rural population to the total maximum rural population
CBR	is the crude birth rate; the number of births per 1000 people
RNI	is the rate of natural increase
OM	is the amount of out-migration
EIM	is the amount of externally generated in-migration
EX	is the amount of excess population; $RP_{s,t}(RNI_{s,t\rightarrow t+10}+1) + EIM_{s,t\rightarrow t+10}(RNI_{s,t\rightarrow t+10}/2 + 1) - MRP_s$
ROM	is the amount of out-migration going to rural areas
%R	is the percent of the population living in rural areas
i	signifies an out-migration state
j	signifies an in-migration state
M	is the unadjusted number of migrants
D	is the distance between two states
N-S	is the absolute value of the difference in latitude between two states
E-W	is a dummy variable taking a value of one if a potential receiving state is west of the out-migration state and a value of zero if it is not
AM	is the adjusted number of migrants
RIM	is the amount of rural in-migration

This relatively simple model has two main parts: the first dealing with the natural increase of the population and the second with the redistribution of the population across states. While severe data limitations prevent the estimation and use of a more sophisticated model, the present effort does represent a first attempt to utilize the scattered available information relating to U.S. demographic history in such a way as to quantitatively evaluate a number of important, yet previously untested, hypotheses concerning the course of U.S. population growth. As new research fills the gaps in our knowledge of fertility, migration, and especially mortality trends, the settlement model could be altered in order to take advantage of additional information which would allow the model to better approximate reality.

The natural increase section of the model is represented by Equations (1) through (4). A detailed description of the theory and methods underlying these equations can be found in Chapters II and III. Briefly, Equations (1) and (2) were estimated using land availability measures as independent variables in explaining the cross-section and time-series variation in the child-woman ratio and the proportion of the population consisting of females of reproductive age. Data on the rural white birth ratio for each of the five decade years during the period 1800–1840 were used in the estimation of Equation (1) while data on the proportion of reproductive females for each of the eight decade years during the period 1800–1870 were used in estimating Equation (2). Since the same units (individual states) are followed over time, an error-components, generalized least-squares estimation procedure was used.

The land availability measures are population density variables. As the rural population approaches its maximum value (either for a given state or for the entire region), land becomes more scarce while the availability of land increases as the ratio of rural population to maximum rural population falls. Thus, population density and land availability are inversely related.

The buildup of population is hypothesized to lead both to an increase in the price of farmland and to a decline in the rate of return on capital. These changes made it more difficult for parents to provide farms for their children which, in light of the strong northern tradition of multigeniture, presumably led to a decline in the demand for surviving children. The resulting change in marital customs and decline in marital fertility is partially offset by an increase in the proportion of women in their childbearing ages which accompanies higher settlement levels. The predicted values from Equations (1) and (2) are combined along with an adjustment factor which takes into consideration intra-decade population growth, infant and child mortality, and under-enumeration as crude birth rate estimates by state and by decade are produced by Equation (3). Finally, after adopting a value of 22 as the crude death rate, estimates of the rate of natural increase over the decade are calculated in Equation (4).

The migration section consists of Equations (5) through (10). In Equation (5), the population of each state (allowing for the estimated amount of natural growth and for in-migration from certain areas outside of the 23-state area) is compared to the maximum value.[2] If the maximum is exceeded, the difference equals the amount of out-migration. If, instead, the population is less than the maximum, there is no out-migration.[3] In Equation (6), the percentage of the population residing in rural areas is used to allocate out-migration between rural and urban destination areas. Equation (7) divides the states into in-migration states (the j's) and out-migration states (the i's) and a gravity-type model (Equation (8)), described in Chapters IV and V, is used to distribute the migration stream.[4] Briefly, migration from i to j increases if j is west of i (reflecting higher quality available land in the west compared with land in the east which had been passed over during the settlement process), and as the relative amount of available land in j increases (indicating a higher return from out-migration), the total distance (representing monetary, psychic and information costs) and the latitudinal distance (reflecting climatic similarities and latitude-specific human capital for farmers) between the two states decrease, and the total amount of out-migration from i (a scale factor) increases. Equation (9) imposes an adding-up constraint by using a proportional error adjustment, and Equation (10) computes the adjusted amount of in-migration.

The final equation (Equation (11)) combines the predicted values from the natural increase and migration sections (including in-migration from areas external to the rural north). This completes the estimates for the decade lasting from time t to time t+10. Among the important demographic variables that are estimated are the birth rate by state, the number of people leaving rural areas of each state who migrate either to urban or to other rural areas, and the rural population of each state at the end of the decade. The last estimate is then used to compute the values of the density measures for use in the operation of the model for the decade lasting from time t+10 to time t+20. This process continues until the end of the 1890–1900 decade unless each of the states reaches its maximum population before that date.

A central feature of this approach is that the critical independent variables, measures of the availability of land, are themselves functions of population growth and, thus, are endogneous.[5] If the model were specified so that it could be used to make an entirely self-generating set of forecasts concerning fertility, migration and population growth, the model would be completely closed. Yet, this would require that all of the independent variables were also dependent variables, implying that everyone born within rural areas of the 23-state area spends his/her entire lifetime either within rural areas of his/her state of origin or within rural areas of one of the other 22 states. Thus, there would be no allowance either for out-migration into urban or rural areas outside of the area under consideration or for out-migration into urban sections within this area. At the same time, in-migration from rural or urban areas outside of the 23 states (including areas outside of the United States) and in-migration from urban areas within the 23-state group would be ignored.

In order to address these concerns, some out-migration is allocated to urban areas using the percent rural variable which is entered exogenously (see Equation (6)). In addition, in-migration enters the region, mainly from Europe but also from the South (see Equations (5) and (11)). Still, neither urban-rural migration nor migration out of the region are allowed. While there was little out-migration to areas outside of the United States and little in-migration to rural areas from urban areas either within or outside the 23-state group, by the end of the period under examination out-migration to states outside of the set of 23 states was becoming increasingly important. Ignoring this fact should bias upward the estimated rate of population growth as the period draws to an end.

In sum, assumptions on which a completely closed model rely have little basis in reality. Therefore, the settlement model is not completely self-contained. Nevertheless, the structure of the model is such that changes in any segment of the model can be traced through the system of equations and the long-run repercussions of changes in any of the variables in the model can be examined with regard to any of the other variables.

The model (referred to as Model 1) is used to reproduce the pattern of rural settlement in the northern United States with the results analyzed both at the aggregate and state-specific level. This produces a control solution which is contrasted with the results from alternative growth scenarios. Specifically, by altering the structure of the model, the effects on the settlement process of three seemingly important features of U.S. demographic history are examined. These are the inflow of European immigrants (Model 2), rural to urban migration (Model 3), and the rural fertility decline (Model 4). In this way, the settlement model is used to gain insight into determining which factors had been responsible for the pattern of settlement which characterized the history of the rural northern United States and, in addition, it is used to predict what would have happened if these factors had either taken a different form or had not been present.

VI.2 THE CONTROL SOLUTION—REPLICATING THE COURSE OF U.S. SETTLEMENT

The goal of the control solution is to replicate the actual settlement pattern in rural areas within the group of 23 states, both for the group as a whole and for the individual states. While the results are somewhat mixed, the settlement model is quite successful in certain important instances.

Table VI.1 presents the actual rural population and total density values along with those values predicted by Model 1. The earliest prediction slightly overestimates the total rural population while subsequent predictions are underestimates. The percentage error peaks at 10.6% in 1840, falls to 2.9% in 1870 and, after an increase in 1880, falls during the remaining

Table VI.1. Actual versus Model 1 Rural Population Predictions Aggregated across the 23 Northern States, 1790–1900

	Actual		*Model 1*		*Difference*	
	Rural Pop.[a]	*% of Max.*	*Rural Pop.*[a]	*% of Max.*	*Absolute*[a]	*%*
1790	2,173.8	8.5	2,173.8	8.5	0.0	0.0
1800	2,821.3	11.0	2,910.4	11.4	89.1	3.2
1810	3,803.1	14.9	3,787.0	14.8	−16.1	−0.4
1820	5,143.4	20.1	4,825.9	18.9	−317.5	−6.2
1830	6,759.1	26.4	6,216.2	24.3	−542.9	−8.0
1840	9,156.5	35.8	8,181.9	32.0	−974.6	−10.6
1850	11,714.8	45.8	11,022.8	43.1	−692.0	−5.9
1860	15,180.2	59.3	14,543.2	56.8	−637.0	−4.2
1870	17,709.3	69.2	17,196.6	67.2	−512.7	−2.9
1880	20,959.5	81.9	19,594.0	76.6	−1,365.5	−6.5
1890	22,777.3	89.0	22,197.6	86.8	−579.7	−2.5
1900	23,999.4	93.8	23.520.5	91.9	−478.9	−2.0

Note: [a]in thousands.
Source: Actual Values; Calculated from Table 20, Vol. I, Part 1, U.S. Census, 1960.

two decades. The 1900 error, 478,900 out of an actual population of about 24 million, equals only 2.0% of the actual value.

The aggregate population predictions indicate that the model tracks reasonably well throughout the period under examination. Further, Table VI.2 compares weighted average crude birth rate forecasts from Model 1 with estimates produced by entering actual density values into the fertility section of the model. These values correspond favorably with the largest error being a 10.9% overestimate during the 1880–1890 decade and the smallest errors equaling 0.6% for 1790–1800 and 0.7% for 1840–1850.[6]

These aggregate predictions are based on thousands of state-specific population, fertility, and migration predictions. Table VI.3, which contains a comparison between the actual and predicted internal density values for each state at each time, presents some of these data.[7] While predicted growth rates for some states are quite accurate, for others they are either too fast or too slow. For instance, the predicted rates of rural settlement for states such as Maine, New Hampshire and Vermont com-

Table VI.2. Actual versus Model 1 Rural Crude Birth Rate Predictions Aggregated across the 23 Northern States, 1790–1800 to 1890–1900

	Actual[a]	*Model 1*	*% Difference*
1790–1800	54.1	54.4	0.6
1800–1810	52.4	51.8	−1.1
1810–1820	52.6	49.5	−5.9
1820–1830	50.9	47.9	−5.9
1830–1840	47.0	46.2	−1.7
1840–1850	44.0	44.3	0.7
1850–1860	41.4	41.8	1.0
1860–1870	36.3	37.0	1.9
1870–1880	32.8	33.8	3.0
1880–1890	27.4	30.4	10.9
1890–1900	23.8	25.5	7.1

Note: [a]Actual density values were used in the fertility model.

pare favorably with the actual growth rates, while Model 1 overestimates the rate of settlement for other New England states such as Massachusetts and Connecticut, and underestimates the rate of settlement for midwestern states such as Indiana and Illinois. The general pattern is that predictions of rural population growth for the states which had been settled first (during the beginning of the nineteenth century) are too high; predictions for the states which had been settled next (in the middle part of the nineteenth century) are too low; and for the states which had been settled last (in the second half of the nineteenth century), the predicted rates of population growth are once again, for the most part, overestimated.

It is interesting to note that Model 1 does a good job of predicting the date in which the settlement process began in several of the states which were settled during the second half of the nineteenth century. All states are considered in the analysis during each decade and the reason that states such as Minnesota and Iowa have predicted internal density values of zero for the first couple of decades is that Model 1 predicts zero in-migration for these states. Over time, the model allocates some of the out-migration flow into these and other late developing states, and continued in-migration along with the natural in-

Table VI.3. Actual versus Predicted Internal Density Values from Model 1 for Each of the 23 Northern States, 1790–1900

	Maine		*New Hampshire*		*Vermont*		*Massachusetts*		*Rhode Island*		*Connecticut*	
t	*Act.*	*Pred.*	*Act.*	*Pred.*	*Act.*	*Pred.*	*Act.*	*Pred.*	*Act.*	*Pred.*	*Act.*	*Pred.*
1900	—	—	—	—	—	—	—	—	—	—	—	—
1890	—	—	—	—	—	—	—	—	—	—	1.00	—
1880	—	—	—	—	—	—	—	—	—	—	.99	—
1870	—	—	—	—	—	—	—	—	—	—	.98	—
1860	1.00	1.00	—	—	—	—	1.00	—	—	—	.92	—
1850	.96	.99	1.00	—	1.00	—	.99	—	—	—	.85	—
1840	.88	.78	.97	—	.95	1.00	.92	—	—	—	.74	—
1830	.74	.61	.97	—	.91	.94	.85	—	1.00	—	.74	—
1820	.55	.46	.90	1.00	.76	.71	.81	—	.96	—	.69	1.00
1810	.42	.34	.79	.85	.71	.50	.75	1.00	.88	—	.67	.99
1800	.28	.25	.68	.67	.50	.37	.72	.83	.82	1.00	.65	.80
1790	.18	.18	.52	.52	.28	.28	.66	.66	.83	.83	.63	.63

	New York		*New Jersey*		*Pennsylvania*		*Delaware*		*Maryland*		*Ohio*	
t	*Act.*	*Pred.*	*Act.*	*Pred.*	*Act.*	*Pred.*	*Act.*	*Pred.*	*Act.*	*Pred.*	*Act.*	*Pred.*
1900	—	—	1.00	—	1.00	—	.94	—	.94	—	—	—
1890	—	—	.97	—	.95	—	.93	—	.86	—	—	—
1880	—	—	.93	—	.88	—	.93	—	.83	—	1.00	—
1870	—	—	.92	—	.77	1.00	.89	—	.76	—	.91	1.00
1860	1.00	—	.82	—	.70	.99	.86	—	.71	—	.89	.84
1850	.94	1.00	.73	—	.62	.82	.74	—	.62	—	.80	.57

1840	.83	.93	.60	1.00	.50	.63	.66	—	.56	—	.66	.26
1830	.69	.58	.55	.96	.40	.48	.73	—	.56	1.00	.42	.10
1820	.51	.40	.49	.76	.32	.35	.69	1.00	.54	.98	.26	.01
1810	.36	.27	.43	.58	.25	.26	.69	.90	.52	.80	.11	.00
1800	.22	.19	.38	.44	.19	.19	.61	.72	.49	.63	.02	.00
1790	.13	.13	.33	.33	.14	.14	.56	.56	.48	.48	.00	.00

	Indiana		*Illinois*		*Michigan*		*Wisconsin*		*Minnesota*		*Iowa*	
t	*Act.*	*Pred.*	*Act.*	*Pred.*	*Act.*	*Pred.*	*Act.*	*Pred.*	*Act.*	*Pred.*	*Act.*	*Pred.*
1900	1.00	—	1.00	.94	.99	—	.92	—	.86	.72	1.00	—
1890	.97	1.00	.96	.79	.92	—	.82	1.00	.65	.53	.91	1.00
1880	.96	.86	.97	.56	.83	—	.72	.80	.47	.33	.83	.77
1870	.87	.62	.88	.36	.64	1.00	.61	.56	.28	.20	.63	.54
1860	.75	.39	.67	.20	.44	.88	.48	.33	.12	.10	.37	.31
1850	.57	.18	.36	.09	.25	.41	.20	.12	.00	.03	.11	.11
1840	.41	.06	.21	.03	.14	.08	.02	.02	.00	.01	.03	.02
1830	.21	.02	.07	.01	.02	.03	.00	.01	.00	.00	.00	.01
1820	.09	.01	.03	.00	.01	.01	.00	.00	.00	.00	.00	.00
1810	.01	.00	.01	.00	.00	.00	.00	.00	.00	.00	.00	.00
1800	.00	.00	.00	.00	.00	.00	.00	.00	.00	.00	.00	.00
1790	.00	.00	.00	.00	.00	.00	.00	.00	.00	.00	.00	.00

(continued)

Table VI.3. (Continued)

t	Missouri		North Dakota		South Dakota		Nebraska		Kansas	
	Act.	Pred.	Act.	Pred.	Act.	Pred.	Act.	Pred.	Act.	Pred.
1900	1.00	.59	.52	.78	.64	1.00	.91	.97	—	.49
1890	.92	.44	.32	.56	.57	.97	.86	.79	1.00	.36
1880	.82	.29	.06	.35	.16	.73	.44	.55	.77	.23
1870	.65	.18	.00	.22	.02	.50	.11	.36	.27	.14
1860	.50	.10	.00	.11	.00	.29	.03	.20	.08	.08
1850	.30	.05	.00	.04	.00	.10	.00	.08	.00	.04
1840	.19	.02	.00	.01	.00	.02	.00	.02	.00	.02
1830	.07	.01	.00	.00	.00	.01	.00	.01	.00	.01
1820	.03	.00	.00	.00	.00	.00	.00	.00	.00	.00
1810	.01	.00	.00	.00	.00	.00	.00	.00	.00	.00
1800	.00	.00	.00	.00	.00	.00	.00	.00	.00	.00
1790	.00	.00	.00	.00	.00	.00	.00	.00	.00	.00

Source: Actual Values; Calculated from Table 20, Vol. I, Part 1, U.S. Census, 1960.

crease of the population leads to the eventual growth of the rural population. Thus, the success of this model in predicting the starting date of the build-up of the population for several of the states further attests to the predictive power of Model 1.

However, it is clear that the predicted settlement dates and rates of population growth for a number of states deviate significantly from the actual values. This is not surprising given the structure of the model. While a number of state-specific measures are included as independent variables in the model, there are particular aspects of certain states which have gone unmeasured. For example, the underestimation of the early growth of the rural population in Ohio may be due to the system of canals which had been built in Ohio around the time of its settlement. Thus, the distance variable, acting as a proxy for transportation costs, failed to consider the role that these canals had played in making transportation to and within Ohio less expensive and, in total, making Ohio a more desirable destination state. The railroad was another factor which reduced the ability of the distance variable to measure migration and marketing costs. It follows that, during the middle part of the century, the model underestimates population growth in Missouri, a state with relatively good railroad access, while overestimating population growth in North Dakota, South Dakota and Nebraska, states with limited railroad access. Further, the settlement of particular states was affected by the Civil War, the Homestead Act, and by cyclical movements in economic activity (out-migration to rural areas on the frontier is likely to have increased during periods of depressed industrial growth).

While these examples demonstrate that improvements in state-specific predictions would accompany the use of finer measures of state characteristics, it is the aggregate predictions which are of primary interest for the purposes of this study. A reasonably accurate replication of total U.S. population growth in rural areas of the 23 states has demonstrated the applicability of the model as well as the consistency between its different components.

This can be further seen by examining the regional settlement predictions presented in Table VI.4. For New England, predicted population levels are above the actual levels as the actual buildup of the population took place about a decade slower than that predicted by Model 1 (for example, the pre-

Table VI.4. Actual versus Predicted Rural Population Values from Model 1 Aggregated by Region, 1790 to 1900

	New England[a]				Middle Atlantic +[b]				East North Central[c]				West North Central[d]			
	Actual		Predicted		Actual		Predicted		Actual		Predicted		Actual		Predicted	
t	Rural Pop.[e]	% of Max Value	Rural Pop.[e]	% of Max Value	Rural Pop.[e]	% of Max Value	Rural Pop.[e]	% of Max Value	Rural Pop.[e]	% of Max Value	Rural Pop.[e]	% of Max Value	Rural Pop.[e]	% of Max Value	Rural Pop.[e]	% of Max Value
1900	—	—	—	—	6,074.7	100.0	—	—	8,765.6	100.0	8,767.1	100.0	7,402.1	100.0	6,219.0	100.0
1890	—	—	—	—	5,978.1	98.4	—	—	8,366.4	95.4	8,440.8	96.3	6,626.0	89.5	5,222.4	84.0
1880	—	—	—	—	5,886.4	96.9	—	—	8,126.6	92.7	7,411.9	84.5	5,039.1	68.1	3,647.8	58.7
1870	—	—	—	—	5,492.1	90.4	6,506.8	100.0	7,152.8	81.6	6,258.5	71.4	3,125.9	42.2	2,403.8	38.7
1860	1,986.8	100.0	2,027.5	100.0	5,364.8	88.3	6,484.9	99.7	5,953.4	67.9	4,670.3	53.3	1,880.0	25.4	1,360.5	21.9
1850	1,943.5	97.8	2,023.6	99.8	4,869.0	80.2	5,979.2	91.9	4,114.1	46.9	2,496.1	28.5	790.0	10.7	523.8	8.4
1840	1,800.9	90.6	1,910.7	94.2	4,133.3	68.0	5,284.3	81.2	2.811.8	32.1	856.3	9.8	410.3	5.5	130.7	2.1
1830	1,680.0	84.6	1,805.3	89.0	3,509.5	57.8	4,018.2	61.8	1.433.4	16.4	337.0	3.8	135.5	1.8	55.6	0.9
1820	1,485.1	74.7	1,654.5	81.6	2,808.6	46.2	3,106.2	47.7	783.1	8.9	51.8	0.6	66.6	0.9	13.4	0.2
1810	1,323.3	66.6	1,483.2	73.2	2,190.1	36.1	2,299.1	35.3	269.8	3.1	3.7	0.0	19.8	0.3	0.9	0.0
1800	1,131.6	57.0	1,199.3	59.2	1,638.8	27.0	1,710.9	26.3	51.0	0.6	0.2	0.0	0.0	0.0	0.0	0.0
1790	933.2	47.0	933.2	46.0	1,240.6	20.4	1,240.6	19.1	0.0	0.0	0.0	0.0	0.0	0.0	0.0	0.0

Notes: [a]Maine, New Hampshire, Vermont, Massachusetts, Rhode Island, Connecticut
[b]New York, New Jersey, Pennsylvania, Delaware, Maryland
[c]Ohio, Indiana, Illinois, Michigan, Wisconsin
[d]Minnesota, Iowa, Missouri, North Dakota, South Dakota, Nebraska, Kansas
[e]in thousands.

Source: Actual Values; Calculated from Table 20, Vol. I, Part 1, U.S. Census, 1960.

dicted value for 1810 is approximately equal to the actual value for 1820). The predictions for the Middle Atlantic States (plus Maryland and Delaware) are also somewhat too large, particularly after 1820. The actual increase in the population was slower by amounts ranging from under ten years in 1830 to a 1860 prediction which is in excess of the actual 1900 maximum (this is due to the fact that the model assumes that states retain their maximum population levels while, in reality, some limited short-term rural de-population took place).

On the other hand, for the East North Central States, the initial population predictions were too low by about ten to twenty years but the difference was less than ten years by 1850 (when the actual population was less than the predicted value for 1860). Finally, the initial population predictions for the West North Central States were about ten years off and, by 1840, the time difference was less than a decade. In total, the results from aggregating the states into regions were encouraging and provide additional evidence that this relatively simple model is successful in reproducing the U.S. population experience, especially at higher levels of aggregation.

An analysis of the state-specific and aggregate results answers several of the questions posed earlier.[8] The date of initial settlement of rural areas of a particular state resulted from the relationship between properties within the state which attracted in-migration and the distance from out-migration states. States which were virtually unsettled offered considerable economic opportunities but, when the distance between an out-migration state and an unsettled state was very large, the costs of migration outweighed the benefits and there was very little in-migration to the unsettled state. Over time, increased settlement of other states diminished the distance between out-migration states and unsettled states and, eventually, the attraction of available land led to the initial settlement of a state.

At first, the buildup of population continued at a moderate rate resulting almost entirely from in-migration. However, as the population base grew, fertility increasingly affected population growth. The availability of land and the presence of high prospective earnings led to a high demand for children and, therefore, to high levels of the rate of natural increase. High fertility levels caused an increase in the rate of population growth which was magnified by continued in-migration resulting from a declining value of the distance variable and a large value of the relative land availability variable. However, as the state reached advanced levels of settlement, economic opportunities were diminished leading to a decline in the demand for children and to a decline in in-migration as the amount of available land decreased. At this point, the rural population of the state grew at a slower rate with low fertility and little in-migration until an excess demand for land was created and, since other less settled states offered greater economic opportunities, out-migration began and a stable rural population resulted. Further, states which had been settled at later dates experienced a more rapid increase in rural population since, as the century progressed, there were more states which were at higher levels of settlement and, therefore, an unsettled state offered greater opportunities compared with the rest of the states in the region. The presence of available land more than compensated for the generally large distances between the settled and the unsettled states as the states farther west were the recipients of out-migration from the east. Thus, the fact that the basic pattern of settlement was condensed over time was predicted by the settlement model.

The results indicate that demographic variables reacted to changes in economic opportunities associated with population growth. The settlement of the rural north led to a decline in the availability of land, and, therefore, to a reduction in fertility rates, a shift from net in-migration to net out-migration and an increase in both rural-urban and east-west migration. The settlement process, through its effect on the economic environment, led directly to the decline in fertility and to the changes in migration which characterized the demographic history of the United States. In turn, it was the movement in demographic variables which led to the eventual reduction in the rate of rural population growth within states.

VI.3 ALTERNATIVE SCENARIOS: THE IMPACTS OF EUROPEAN IMMIGRATION, RURAL-URBAN MIGRATION AND THE RURAL FERTILITY DECLINE

The significance of European immigration, rural-urban migration, and the rural fertility decline with respect to rural settlement can be examined through the analysis of the counterfactual results generated by changing the structure of the settlement model. The role of European immigration in accounting for rural northern population growth can be determined by limiting the source of external in-migration (EIM in Equations (5) and (11)) to the southern states. The resulting alternative model, referred to as Model 2, will be the basis of the first alternative scenario. If there had been no rural-urban migration, the scenario presented in Model 3, then all of the out-migration predicted in the model would have been allocated among rural areas. In terms of the various equations which comprise the model, %R in Equation (6) takes the value of one for all t. Finally, while most other nations experienced a fertility decline only after mortality conditions had become more favorable, the U.S. appears to have had almost a century of declining fertility in the face of stable mortality. The significance of the fertility decline will be explored in the third alternative scenario where Equations (1) through (3) are replaced by the crude birth rate predictions from Model 1 for each state either in 1790 or during the decade in which 10% of their rural population had been settled.[9] This model will be referred to as Model 4.

Table VI.5 compares the rural population estimates from the control solution with the estimates from the first alternative model.[10] Columns (6) and (7) show that European immigration had little effect on rural northern population growth during the first half of the nineteenth century. In 1830, for example, the absence of European immigration would have lowered the rural population of the 23 states by only about 279,000 out of over 6.2 million (a decrease of 4.5%). However, by 1870, the absence of European immigration would have had a much greater effect, lowering the population by 26.3%, from about 17.2 million to under 12.7 million. The percentage impact of European immigration remained around this level for the rest of the period.

While immigration had a sizable effect on rural population growth in the northern states (at least during the second half of the nineteenth century), rural to urban migration had only a limited effect.[11] As late as 1840, the elimination of rural to urban migration would have only raised the rural population by under 100,000 people or 1.2% (Columns (10) and (11)). While this percentage increased as the century progressed, in

Table VI.5. Model 1, Model 2, Model 3 and Model 4 Rural Population Predictions Aggregated across the 23 Northern States, 1790 to 1900

	Model 1		*Model 2*		*Difference: Model 2 Vs. Model 1*		*Model 3*		*Difference: Model 3 Vs. Model 1*		*Model 4*		*Difference: Model 4 Vs. Model 1*	
	Rural Pop.[a]	*% of Max.*	*Rural Pop.*[a]	*% of Max.*	*Absolute*[a]	*%*	*Rural Pop.*[a]	*% of Max.*	*Absolute*[a]	*%*	*Rural Pop.*[a]	*% of Max.*	*Absolute*[a]	*%*
1790	2,173.8	8.5	2,173.8	8.5	0.0	0.0	2,173.8	8.5	0.0	0.0	2,173.8	8.5	0.0	0.0
1800	2,910.4	11.4	2,872.2	11.2	−38.2	−1.3	2,910.5	11.4	0.1	0.0	2,910.4	11.4	0.0	0.0
1810	3,787.0	14.8	3,714.8	14.5	−72.2	−1.9	3,788.9	14.8	1.9	0.1	3,869.4	15.1	82.4	2.2
1820	4,825.9	18.9	4,679.4	18.3	−146.5	−3.0	4,843.0	18.9	17.1	0.4	5,158.4	20.2	332.5	6.9
1830	6,216.2	24.3	5,937.7	23.2	−278.5	−4.5	6,261.2	24.5	45.0	0.7	7,079.1	27.7	862.9	13.9
1840	8,181.9	32.0	7,465.6	29.2	−716.3	−8.8	8,281.4	32.4	99.5	1.2	10,050.0	39.3	1,868.1	22.8
1850	11,022.8	43.1	9,350.2	36.5	−1,672.6	−15.2	11,380.7	44.5	357.9	3.2	14,749.8	57.7	3,727.0	33.8
1860	14,543.2	56.8	11,149.0	43.6	−3,394.2	−23.3	15,393.2	60.2	850.0	5.8	21,333.9	83.4	6,790.7	46.7
1870	17,196.6	67.2	12,680.7	49.6	−4,515.9	−26.3	18,428.7	72.0	1,232.1	7.2	25,584.4	100.0	8,387.8	48.8
1880	19,594.0	76.6	14,211.3	55.5	−5,382.7	−27.5	21,213.6	82.9	1,619.6	8.3	—	—	—	—
1890	22,197.6	86.8	15,732.5	61.5	−6,465.1	−29.1	24,223.9	94.7	2,026.3	9.1	—	—	—	—
1900	23,520.5	91.9	17,299.4	67.6	−6,221.1	−26.4	25,584.4	100.0	2,063.9	8.8	—	—	—	—

Note: [a]in thousands.

1900 the population would have been less than 10% larger if there had been no migration from rural to urban areas. In total, the population in the area under examination at the end of the nineteenth century would have been more than one quarter less if there had been no European immigration into this area and under one tenth greater if there had been no urban leakage.

These numbers would have been larger if fertility changes did not have a mediating effect. In the case of no European immigration, the resulting slowdown in the deterioration in economic conditions in rural areas would have led to a larger demand for children and a higher weighed average crude birth rate during the latter part of the century (Table VI.6).[12] By 1870–1880, the crude birth rate would have been 10.9% higher in the absence of European immigration and, by 1890–1900, the crude birth rate would have been greater by more than one third. The crude birth rate would have reacted to the absence of rural to urban migration in an opposite manner. Rural-urban migration was a type of safety valve, slowing the rate of deterioration in rural farm earnings. If there had been no rural to urban migration, poorer economic conditions would have led to a decrease in the demand for children and the crude

Table VI.6. Model 1, Model 2 and Model 3 Rural Crude Birth Rate Predictions Aggregated across the 23 Northern States, 1790–1800 to 1890–1900

	Model 1	*Model 2*	*% Diff.*[a]	*Model 3*	*% Diff.*[a]
1790–1800	54.4	54.4	0.0	54.4	0.0
1800–1810	51.8	51.8	0.0	51.8	0.0
1810–1820	49.5	49.5	0.0	49.5	0.0
1820–1830	47.9	48.0	0.2	47.9	0.0
1830–1840	46.2	46.8	1.3	46.2	0.0
1840–1850	44.3	45.0	1.6	44.3	0.0
1850–1860	41.8	41.8	0.0	41.8	0.0
1860–1870	37.0	38.8	4.9	36.3	−1.9
1870–1880	33.8	37.5	10.9	32.3	−4.4
1880–1890	30.4	36.4	19.7	28.1	−7.6
1890–1900	25.5	35.2	38.0	23.5	−7.8

Note: [a]Percent difference between the crude birth rate predictions from the alternative model and the control solution (Model 1).

birth rate would have been 7.8% lower by the final decade of the century.[13]

The finding that birth rates fell due to immigration and rose due to urban leakage demonstrates the degree to which people responded to changes in the economic environment and illustrates the role that birth rates played in regulating the rate of population growth. The importance of the fertility response is vividly shown in the results from Model 4. The last two columns of Table VI.5 show that the decline in rural fertility had a major impact on the growth in rural population.[14] Had birth rates in the United States followed the pattern in most of the rest of the world by remaining stable until mortality conditions improved, then the rural population of the northern states would have increased at a much more rapid rate than actually occurred. This can be seen by examining the population value for 1870. If birth rates had not fallen, the population would have been larger by almost 50%, by far the greatest effect found in the three alternative scenarios.[15] Thus, it can be concluded that, while European immigration, rural to urban migration and the decline in rural fertility all affected rural population growth, it was the rural fertility decline which, by far, was the most significant of the three in terms of explaining the growth of the rural population within the 23-state area. Moreover, the fertility decline is endogenously determined within the settlement model while immigration and the distribution of the migration flow between rural and urban areas are not. The result that immigration and rural-urban migration were less important factors in the settlement process implies that their exogeneity is less problematic than if they had played a larger role.

VI.4 CONCLUSION

The preceding analysis indicates that the rural fertility decline was a reaction to increased population pressure which played a major role in retarding the growth of the population and in accounting for the observed pattern of population distribution in the rural northern United States. In this way, population growth itself initiated a demographic response which, in turn, dictated the course of further population growth.

As discussed in Chapter III, the idea that a relationship exists between population pressure and demographic change is not new, particularly in the analysis of U.S. demographic history. Turner advanced the notion that westward migration in the United States had acted as a safety valve by dissipating the pressures of overpopulation which had led to social upheaval in other nations throughout the world.[16] This idea is easily extended to rural-urban migration since urban areas, as was the case with rural areas in the West, attracted "excess" population from overcrowded rural areas in the East and Mid-West.[17]

Both of these safety valves are incorporated into the settlement model. Overpopulation in the East led to out-migration into areas in the West, and the predicted pattern of rural population growth was, in part, dependent on changes in the predicted amount of westward migration which led to the settlement of new states. This is shown in Table VI.7 where the predicted amount of rural-rural migration in the control solu-

Table VI.7. Model 1, Model 2, Model 3 and Model 4 Rural-Rural Migration Predictions Aggregated across the 23 Northern States, 1790–1800 to 1890–1900

	Model 1[a]	*Model 2*[a]	*% Diff.*[b]	*Model 3*[a]	*% Diff.*[b]	*Model 4*[a]	*% Diff.*[b]
1790–1800	1.2	1.2	0.0	1.2	0.0	1.1	−8.3
1800–1810	16.0	16.1	0.6	17.9	11.9	42.1	163.1
1810–1820	151.0	151.6	0.4	166.0	9.9	316.3	109.5
1820–1830	272.0	274.2	0.8	296.5	9.0	593.4	118.2
1830–1840	335.9	341.0	1.5	386.9	15.2	1,076.7	220.5
1840–1850	1,484.0	335.6	−77.4	1,738.9	17.2	2,995.0	101.8
1850–1860	2,154.5	321.7	−85.1	2,620.0	21.6	5,271.5	144.7
1860–1870	1,610.7	569.1	−64.7	2,034.7	26.3	5,661.2	251.5
1870–1880	1,294.0	632.1	−51.2	1,682.4	30.0	—	—
1880–1890	1,678.0	559.1	−66.7	3,127.7	86.4	—	—
1890–1900	785.7	404.0	−48.6	1,898.7	141.7	—	—

Notes: [a]in thousands
[b]percent difference between the rural-rural migration predictions from the alternative model and the control solution (Model 1).

tion increased during most of the period with the increase in the values of the density variables (until the effect of declining fertility led to less out-migration). Further, this table also shows that, if out-migration to urban areas had not taken place (Model 3), an increase in rural-rural migration would have accompanied the increase in the rate of rural population growth. On the other hand, if there had been no European immigration (Model 2), rural-rural migration would have been less. Similarly, Table VI.8 shows that rural-urban migration increased over time in the control solution (except for the final decade) but it would have been less if there had been no European immigration.

However, there was an additional safety valve which played a prominent role in this study: the decline in rural fertility. While the second alternative scenario (Model 3) resulted in rural-rural migration replacing some of the rural-urban migration, another effect was an increase in the rate of decline in fertility rates. On the other hand, in Model 2, when European immigration was ignored, rural population pressures were reduced and fertility fell at a slower rate. Thus, fertility can be thought of as an additional safety valve for dissipating population pressure.

Table VI.8. Model 1, Model 2 and Model 4 Rural-Urban Migration Predictions Aggregated across the 23 Northern States, 1790–1800 to 1890–1900

	Model 1[a]	*Model 2*[a]	*% Diff.*[b]	*Model 4*[a]	*% Diff.*[b]
1790–1800	0.1	0.1	0.0	0.1	0.0
1800–1810	1.9	1.9	0.0	4.9	157.9
1810–1820	14.8	14.8	0.0	30.9	108.8
1820–1830	24.3	24.5	0.8	53.0	118.1
1830–1840	46.2	46.9	1.5	148.2	220.8
1840–1850	243.6	55.1	−77.4	491.6	101.8
1850–1860	453.9	67.8	−85.1	1,110.5	144.7
1860–1870	497.5	175.8	−64.7	1,748.7	251.5
1870–1880	520.9	254.4	−51.2	—	—
1880–1890	960.4	320.0	−66.7	—	—
1890–1900	630.0	323.9	−48.6	—	—

Notes: [a]in thousands

[b]percent difference between the rural-urban migration predictions from the alternative model and the control solution (Model 1).

The importance of this factor was vividly demonstrated in the third alternative scenario (Model 4) where both rural-rural and rural-urban migration increased (Tables VI.7 and VI.8) when fertility no longer reacted to increased population pressure with the overall effect being a sharp increase in rural population growth.

In conclusion, population growth led to the observed movements in demographic factors which eventually brought the growth of the rural population to a halt. Of these movements, the decline in rural fertility was a critical factor, both in acting as a safety valve for population pressure and in determining the course of U.S. demographic history.

VI.5 APPENDIX: ADDITIONAL STATE-SPECIFIC PREDICTIONS

The following tables present supplementary state-specific predictions from Models 1, 2, 3 and 4.

Table VIA.1. Actual versus Model 1 Rural Crude Birth Rate Predictions for Each of the 23 Northern States, 1790–1800 to 1890–1900

	Maine		*New Hampshire*		*Vermont*		*Massachusetts*		*Rhode Island*		*Connecticut*	
t	*Actual*[a]	*Model 1*	*Actual*[a]	*Model 1*	*Actual*[a]	*Model 1*	*Actual*[a]	*Model 1*	*Actual*[a]	*Model 1*	*Actual*[a]	*Model 1*
1890–1900	21.2	22.3	21.2	22.3	21.2	22.3	21.2	22.3	21.2	22.3	21.2	22.3
1880–1890	23.4	25.0	23.4	25.0	23.4	25.0	23.4	25.0	23.4	25.0	23.7	25.0
1870–1880	26.7	27.4	26.7	27.4	26.7	27.4	26.7	27.4	26.7	27.4	27.3	27.4
1860–1870	29.4	29.9	30.5	29.9	29.4	29.9	29.4	29.9	30.5	29.9	31.8	29.9
1850–1860	33.7	33.3	32.4	33.0	32.4	33.0	32.8	33.0	33.0	33.0	36.8	33.0
1840–1850	38.0	41.7	35.5	35.4	36.0	35.4	37.0	35.4	37.0	35.4	41.9	35.4
1830–1840	43.7	47.3	37.3	36.9	39.1	38.5	40.7	36.9	36.4	36.9	43.7	36.9
1820–1830	49.3	51.6	40.4	38.0	44.1	45.7	42.9	38.0	38.8	38.0	45.9	38.0
1810–1820	53.1	54.8	44.1	42.7	46.2	51.2	45.2	38.7	41.9	38.7	47.2	39.1
1800–1810	56.5	57.0	47.5	47.6	51.7	54.4	46.7	43.7	44.0	39.3	48.4	44.5
1790–1800	58.8	58.6	51.7	51.6	56.8	56.7	48.4	48.4	44.3	44.1	49.1	49.1

	New York		*New Jersey*		*Pennsylvania*		*Delaware*		*Maryland*		*Ohio*	
t	*Actual*[a]	*Model 1*	*Actual*[a]	*Model 1*	*Actual*[a]	*Model 1*	*Actual*[a]	*Model 1*	*Actual*[a]	*Model 1*	*Actual*[a]	*Model 1*
1890–1900	21.2	22.3	22.2	22.3	23.0	22.3	23.6	22.3	26.1	22.3	21.2	22.3
1880–1890	23.4	25.0	26.0	25.0	27.5	25.0	25.8	25.0	27.5	25.0	23.4	25.0
1870–1880	26.7	27.4	29.2	27.4	34.1	27.4	30.3	27.4	34.4	27.4	29.6	27.4
1860–1870	29.4	29.9	34.9	29.9	38.6	30.2	33.7	29.9	38.3	29.9	32.8	34.9
1850–1860	34.2	33.0	40.4	33.0	43.5	38.5	40.1	33.0	43.5	33.0	38.4	45.2
1840–1850	39.5	37.5	45.7	35.4	48.2	45.5	44.1	35.4	46.7	35.4	44.1	54.6

1830–1840	44.9	47.9	48.4	38.1	52.1	50.4	43.8	36.9	48.1	36.9	51.5	58.9
1820–1830	50.3	53.0	50.7	44.3	54.5	54.0	45.9	38.0	49.6	38.6	56.0	61.1
1810–1820	54.4	56.2	52.8	49.3	56.7	56.5	46.8	41.3	50.9	44.1	59.6	61.5
1800–1810	57.7	58.2	54.4	52.9	58.2	58.2	49.1	46.4	52.0	48.7	61.4	61.8
1790–1800	59.5	59.6	55.7	55.6	59.3	59.5	50.7	50.6	52.3	52.4	61.9	62.0

	Indiana		*Illinois*		*Michigan*		*Wisconsin*		*Minnesota*		*Iowa*	
t	*Actual*[a]	*Model 1*	*Actual*[a]	*Model 1*	*Actual*[a]	*Model 1*	*Actual*[a]	*Model 1*	*Actual*[a]	*Model 1*	*Actual*[a]	*Model 1*
1890–1900	22.2	22.3	22.6	29.4	24.0	22.3	27.5	22.3	33.1	38.0	24.3	22.3
1880–1890	24.8	29.6	24.4	39.2	29.1	25.0	32.7	31.8	40.6	45.9	29.1	32.7
1870–1880	30.9	39.2	30.6	46.7	38.0	27.4	38.9	41.0	48.4	51.0	38.4	41.8
1860–1870	37.0	47.8	39.5	52.5	45.9	33.7	44.8	49.2	54.2	54.9	47.8	49.7
1850–1860	44.7	55.0	50.2	57.1	53.0	49.3	54.0	56.4	58.8	58.2	56.3	56.5
1840–1850	50.6	58.9	55.2	59.5	56.8	58.5	59.2	59.7	59.8	60.0	59.2	59.7
1830–1840	56.2	60.3	59.2	60.6	60.3	60.1	60.6	60.6	—	—	60.6	60.6
1820–1830	59.5	61.1	60.6	61.2	60.9	61.0	—	—	—	—	—	—
1810–1820	61.5	61.5	61.5	61.5	61.4	61.5	—	—	—	—	—	—
1800–1810	62.0	61.8	62.0	61.8	62.0	61.8	—	—	—	—	—	—
1790–1800	61.9	62.0	—	—	—	—	—	—	—	—	—	—

(*continued*)

Table VIA.1. (Continued)

t	Missouri		North Dakota		South Dakota		Nebraska		Kansas	
	Actual[a]	*Model 1*	*Actual*[a]	*Model 1*	*Actual*[a]	*Model 1*	*Actual*[a]	*Model 1*	*Actual*[a]	*Model 1*
1890–1900	24.0	40.5	43.3	36.9	35.6	23.2	26.1	29.6	21.2	43.0
1880–1890	29.5	47.0	52.2	45.2	49.5	34.0	41.5	39.3	31.1	48.7
1870–1880	37.8	51.5	55.7	50.6	55.0	42.7	52.9	46.7	48.8	52.5
1860–1870	44.3	54.9	57.0	54.7	57.0	50.3	56.3	52.5	55.2	55.5
1850–1860	51.6	57.9	58.8	58.2	58.8	56.7	58.8	57.3	58.8	58.2
1840–1850	55.6	59.7	—	—	—	—	—	—	—	—
1830–1840	59.2	60.6	—	—	—	—	—	—	—	—
1820–1830	60.6	61.2	—	—	—	—	—	—	—	—
1810–1820	61.5	61.5	—	—	—	—	—	—	—	—
1800–1810	—	—	—	—	—	—	—	—	—	—
1790–1800	—	—	—	—	—	—	—	—	—	—

Note: [a]Actual density values were used in the fertility model.

Table VIA.2. Model 1 versus Model 2 Internal Density Predictions for Each of the 23 Northern States, 1790–1900

	Maine		*New Hampshire*		*Vermont*		*Massachusetts*		*Rhode Island*		*Connecticut*	
t	*Model 1*	*Model 2*	*Model 1*	*Model 2*	*Model 1*	*Model 2*	*Model 1*	*Model 2*	*Model 1*	*Model 2*	*Model 1*	*Model 2*
1900	—	—	—	—	—	—	—	—	—	—	—	—
1890	—	—	—	—	—	—	—	—	—	—	—	—
1880	—	—	—	—	—	—	—	—	—	—	—	—
1870	—	—	—	—	—	—	—	—	—	—	—	—
1860	1.00	1.00	—	—	—	—	—	—	—	—	—	—
1850	.99	.95	—	—	—	—	—	—	—	—	—	—
1840	.78	.78	—	—	1.00	1.00	—	—	—	—	—	—
1830	.61	.61	—	—	.94	.94	—	—	—	—	—	—
1820	.46	.46	1.00	1.00	.71	.71	—	—	—	—	1.00	1.00
1810	.34	.34	.85	.85	.50	.50	1.00	1.00	—	—	.99	.99
1800	.25	.25	.67	.67	.37	.37	.83	.83	1.00	1.00	.80	.80
1790	.18	.18	.52	.52	.28	.28	.66	.66	.83	.83	.63	.63

	New York		*New Jersey*		*Pennsylvania*		*Delaware*		*Maryland*		*Ohio*	
t	*Model 1*	*Model 2*	*Model 1*	*Model 2*	*Model 1*	*Model 2*	*Model 1*	*Model 2*	*Model 1*	*Model 2*	*Model 1*	*Model 2*
1900	—	—	—	—	—	—	—	—	—	—	—	—
1890	—	—	—	—	—	—	—	—	—	—	—	—
1880	—	—	—	—	—	—	—	—	—	—	—	1.00
1870	—	1.00	—	—	1.00	1.00	—	—	—	—	1.00	.88
1860	—	.96	—	—	.99	.96	—	—	—	—	.84	.72

(*continued*)

Table VIA.2. (Continued)

t	New York		New Jersey		Pennsylvania		Delaware		Maryland		Ohio	
	Model 1	Model 2	Model 1	Model 2	Model 1	Model 2	Model 1	Model 2	Model 1	Model 2	Model 1	Model 2
1850	1.00	.79	—	—	.82	.80	—	—	—	—	.57	.52
1840	.93	.62	1.00	1.00	.63	.63	—	—	—	—	.26	.26
1830	.58	.47	.96	.96	.48	.48	—	—	1.00	1.00	.10	.10
1820	.40	.34	.76	.76	.35	.35	1.00	1.00	.98	.98	.01	.01
1810	.27	.24	.58	.58	.26	.26	.90	.90	.80	.80	.00	.00
1800	.19	.18	.44	.44	.19	.19	.72	.72	.63	.63	.00	.00
1790	.13	.13	.33	.33	.14	.14	.56	.56	.48	.48	.00	.00

t	Indiana		Illinois		Michigan		Wisconsin		Minnesota		Iowa	
	Model 1	Model 2	Model 1	Model 2	Model 1	Model 2	Model 1	Model 2	Model 1	Model 2	Model 1	Model 2
1900	—	.78	.94	.49	—	.89	—	.42	.72	.15	—	.38
1890	1.00	.62	.79	.36	—	.74	1.00	.31	.53	.10	1.00	.28
1880	.86	.45	.56	.24	—	.56	.80	.21	.33	.06	.77	.18
1870	.62	.29	.36	.15	1.00	.37	.56	.12	.20	.04	.54	.11
1860	.39	.17	.20	.09	.88	.21	.33	.06	.10	.02	.31	.06
1850	.18	.11	.09	.05	.41	.13	.12	.04	.03	.01	.11	.04
1840	.06	.06	.03	.03	.08	.08	.02	.02	.01	.01	.02	.02
1830	.02	.02	.01	.01	.03	.03	.01	.01	.00	.00	.01	.01
1820	.01	.01	.00	.00	.01	.01	.00	.00	.00	.00	.00	.00
1810	.00	.00	.00	.00	.00	.00	.00	.00	.00	.00	.00	.00
1800	.00	.00	.00	.00	.00	.00	.00	.00	.00	.00	.00	.00
1790	.00	.00	.00	.00	.00	.00	.00	.00	.00	.00	.00	.00

t	Missouri		North Dakota		South Dakota		Nebraska		Kansas	
	Model 1	*Model 2*	*Model 1*	*Model 2*	*Model 1*	*Model 2*	*Model 1*	*Model 2*	*Model 1*	*Model 2*
1900	.59	.31	.78	.16	1.00	.36	.97	.34	.49	.24
1890	.44	.23	.56	.11	.97	.26	.79	.25	.36	.17
1880	.29	.16	.35	.07	.73	.17	.55	.17	.23	.12
1870	.18	.10	.22	.04	.50	.10	.36	.10	.14	.08
1860	.10	.06	.11	.02	.29	.05	.20	.06	.08	.05
1850	.05	.04	.04	.01	.10	.03	.08	.03	.04	.03
1840	.02	.02	.01	.01	.02	.02	.02	.02	.02	.02
1830	.01	.01	.00	.00	.01	.01	.01	.01	.01	.01
1820	.00	.00	.00	.00	.00	.00	.00	.00	.00	.00
1810	.00	.00	.00	.00	.00	.00	.00	.00	.00	.00
1800	.00	.00	.00	.00	.00	.00	.00	.00	.00	.00
1790	.00	.00	.00	.00	.00	.00	.00	.00	.00	.00

Table VIA.3. Model 1 versus Model 3 Internal Density Predictions for Each of the 23 Northern States, 1790–1900

	Maine		*New Hampshire*		*Vermont*		*Massachusetts*		*Rhode Island*		*Connecticut*	
t	*Model 1*	*Model 3*	*Model 1*	*Model 3*	*Model 1*	*Model 3*	*Model 1*	*Model 3*	*Model 1*	*Model 3*	*Model 1*	*Model 3*
1900	—	—	—	—	—	—	—	—	—	—	—	—
1890	—	—	—	—	—	—	—	—	—	—	—	—
1880	—	—	—	—	—	—	—	—	—	—	—	—
1870	—	—	—	—	—	—	—	—	—	—	—	—
1860	1.00	—	—	—	—	—	—	—	—	—	—	—
1850	.99	1.00	—	—	—	—	—	—	—	—	—	—
1840	.78	.78	—	—	1.00	1.00	—	—	—	—	—	—
1830	.61	.61	—	—	.94	.96	—	—	—	—	—	—
1820	.46	.46	1.00	1.00	.71	.71	—	—	—	—	—	—
1810	.34	.34	.85	.85	.50	.50	1.00	1.00	—	—	1.00	1.00
1800	.25	.25	.67	.67	.37	.37	.83	.83	1.00	1.00	.99	.99
1790	.18	.18	.52	.52	.28	.28	.66	.66	.83	.83	.80	.80
											.63	.63

	New York		*New Jersey*		*Pennsylvania*		*Delaware*		*Maryland*		*Ohio*	
t	*Model 1*	*Model 3*	*Model 1*	*Model 3*	*Model 1*	*Model 3*	*Model 1*	*Model 3*	*Model 1*	*Model 3*	*Model 1*	*Model 3*
1900	—	—	—	—	—	—	—	—	—	—	—	—
1890	—	—	—	—	—	—	—	—	—	—	—	—
1880	—	—	—	—	—	—	—	—	—	—	—	—
1870	—	—	—	—	1.00	—	—	—	—	—	—	—
1860	—	—	—	—	.99	1.00	—	—	—	—	1.00	1.00
											.84	.88

1850	1.00	1.00	—	—	.82	.83	—	—	—	—	.57	.59
1840	.93	.93	1.00	1.00	.63	.64	—	—	—	—	.26	.26
1830	.58	.59	.96	.96	.48	.48	—	—	1.00	1.00	.10	.10
1820	.40	.40	.76	.76	.35	.36	1.00	1.00	.98	.98	.01	.01
1810	.27	.27	.58	.58	.26	.26	.90	.90	.80	.80	.00	.00
1800	.19	.19	.44	.44	.19	.19	.72	.72	.63	.63	.00	.00
1790	.13	.13	.33	.33	.14	.14	.56	.56	.48	.48	.00	.00

	Indiana		Illinois		Michigan		Wisconsin		Minnesota		Iowa	
t	*Model 1*	*Model 3*	*Model 1*	*Model 3*	*Model 1*	*Model 3*	*Model 1*	*Model 3*	*Model 1*	*Model 3*	*Model 1*	*Model 3*
1900	—	—	.94	1.00	—	—	—	—	.72	1.00	—	—
1890	1.00	—	.79	.99	—	—	1.00	1.00	.53	.93	1.00	1.00
1880	.86	1.00	.56	.70	—	—	.80	.94	.33	.43	.77	.91
1870	.62	.77	.36	.46	1.00	—	.56	.68	.20	.26	.54	.65
1860	.39	.45	.20	.24	.88	1.00	.33	.40	.10	.13	.31	.38
1850	.18	.20	.09	.10	.41	.48	.12	.14	.03	.04	.11	.13
1840	.06	.07	.03	.03	.08	.09	.02	.02	.01	.01	.02	.02
1830	.02	.03	.01	.01	.03	.04	.01	.01	.00	.00	.01	.01
1820	.01	.01	.00	.00	.01	.01	.00	.00	.00	.00	.00	.00
1810	.00	.00	.00	.00	.00	.00	.00	.00	.00	.00	.00	.00
1800	.00	.00	.00	.00	.00	.00	.00	.00	.00	.00	.00	.00
1790	.00	.00	.00	.00	.00	.00	.00	.00	.00	.00	.00	.00

(*continued*)

Table VIA.3. *(Continued)*

	Missouri		*North Dakota*		*South Dakota*		*Nebraska*		*Kansas*	
t	*Model 1*	*Model 3*	*Model 1*	*Model 3*	*Model 1*	*Model 3*	*Model 1*	*Model 3*	*Model 1*	*Model 3*
1900	.59	1.00	.78	—	1.00	—	.97	—	.49	1.00
1890	.44	.61	.56	1.00	.97	1.00	.79	1.00	.36	.60
1880	.29	.37	.35	.46	.73	.87	.55	.69	.23	.30
1870	.18	.23	.22	.28	.50	.61	.36	.45	.14	.18
1860	.10	.12	.11	.14	.29	.35	.20	.24	.08	.09
1850	.05	.06	.04	.04	.10	.12	.08	.09	.04	.04
1840	.02	.02	.01	.01	.02	.02	.02	.02	.02	.02
1830	.01	.01	.00	.00	.01	.01	.01	.01	.01	.01
1820	.00	.00	.00	.00	.00	.00	.00	.00	.00	.00
1810	.00	.00	.00	.00	.00	.00	.00	.00	.00	.00
1800	.00	.00	.00	.00	.00	.00	.00	.00	.00	.00
1790	.00	.00	.00	.00	.00	.00	.00	.00	.00	.00

Table VIA.4. Model 1 versus Model 2 Rural Crude Birth Rate Predictions for Each of the 23 Northern States, 1790–1800 to 1890–1900

	Maine		*New Hampshire*		*Vermont*		*Massachusetts*		*Rhode Island*		*Connecticut*	
t	*Model 1*	*Model 2*	*Model 1*	*Model 2*	*Model 1*	*Model 2*	*Model 1*	*Model 2*	*Model 1*	*Model 2*	*Model 1*	*Model 2*
1890–1900	22.3	28.8	22.3	28.8	22.3	28.8	22.3	28.8	22.3	28.8	22.3	28.8
1880–1890	25.0	30.2	25.0	30.2	25.0	30.2	25.0	30.2	25.0	30.2	25.0	30.2
1870–1880	27.4	31.6	27.4	31.6	27.4	31.6	27.4	31.6	27.4	31.6	27.4	31.6
1860–1870	29.9	32.9	29.9	32.9	29.9	32.9	29.9	32.9	29.9	32.9	29.9	32.9
1850–1860	33.3	36.0	33.0	34.4	33.0	34.4	33.0	34.4	33.0	34.4	33.0	34.4
1840–1850	41.7	42.1	35.4	36.0	35.4	36.0	35.4	36.0	35.4	36.0	35.4	36.0
1830–1840	47.3	47.5	36.9	37.1	38.5	38.7	36.9	37.1	36.9	37.1	36.9	37.1
1820–1830	51.6	51.7	38.0	38.1	45.7	45.8	38.0	38.1	38.0	38.1	38.0	38.1
1810–1820	54.8	54.8	42.7	42.8	51.2	51.2	38.7	38.8	38.7	38.8	39.1	39.1
1800–1810	57.0	57.0	47.6	47.6	54.4	54.5	43.7	43.8	39.3	39.4	44.5	44.5
1790–1800	58.6	58.6	51.6	51.6	56.7	56.7	48.4	48.4	44.1	44.1	49.1	49.1

	New York		*New Jersey*		*Pennsylvania*		*Delaware*		*Maryland*		*Ohio*	
t	*Model 1*	*Model 2*	*Model 1*	*Model 2*	*Model 1*	*Model 2*	*Model 1*	*Model 2*	*Model 1*	*Model 2*	*Model 1*	*Model 2*
1890–1900	22.3	28.8	22.3	28.8	22.3	28.8	22.3	28.8	22.3	28.8	22.3	28.8
1880–1890	25.0	30.2	25.0	30.2	25.0	30.2	25.0	30.2	25.0	30.2	25.0	30.2
1870–1880	27.4	31.6	27.4	31.6	27.4	31.6	27.4	31.6	27.4	31.6	27.4	35.1
1860–1870	29.9	34.2	29.9	32.9	30.2	34.3	29.9	32.9	29.9	32.9	34.9	41.0
1850–1860	33.0	40.4	33.0	34.4	38.5	40.2	33.0	34.4	33.0	34.4	45.2	47.7
1840–1850	37.5	46.2	35.4	36.0	45.5	45.9	35.4	36.0	35.4	36.0	54.6	55.0
1830–1840	47.9	50.9	38.1	38.3	50.4	50.6	36.9	37.1	36.9	37.1	58.9	59.0

(*continued*)

Table VIA.4. (Continued)

t	New York		New Jersey		Pennsylvania		Delaware		Maryland		Ohio	
	Model 1	Model 2	Model 1	Model 2	Model 1	Model 2	Model 1	Model 2	Model 1	Model 2	Model 1	Model 2
1820–1830	53.0	54.4	44.3	44.4	54.0	54.1	38.0	38.1	38.6	38.7	61.1	61.2
1810–1820	56.2	56.9	49.3	49.3	56.5	56.5	41.3	41.4	44.1	44.2	61.5	61.6
1800–1810	58.2	58.5	52.9	52.9	58.2	58.3	46.4	46.5	48.7	48.8	61.8	61.8
1790–1800	59.6	59.6	55.6	55.6	59.5	59.5	50.6	50.6	52.4	52.4	62.0	62.0

t	Indiana		Illinois		Michigan		Wisconsin		Minnesota		Iowa	
	Model 1	Model 2	Model 1	Model 2	Model 1	Model 2	Model 1	Model 2	Model 1	Model 2	Model 1	Model 2
1890–1900	22.3	40.4	29.4	47.7	22.3	36.8	22.3	49.1	38.0	54.4	22.3	49.9
1880–1890	29.6	46.4	39.2	51.7	25.0	43.3	31.8	52.6	45.9	56.0	32.7	53.2
1870–1880	39.2	51.4	46.7	54.8	27.4	49.3	41.0	55.4	51.0	57.4	41.8	55.7
1860–1870	47.8	55.0	52.5	57.0	33.7	54.1	49.2	57.5	54.9	58.5	49.7	57.6
1850–1860	55.0	57.3	57.1	58.6	49.3	56.8	56.4	58.9	58.2	59.4	56.5	58.9
1840–1850	58.9	59.2	59.5	59.8	58.5	58.8	59.7	60.0	60.0	60.3	59.7	60.0
1830–1840	60.3	60.4	60.6	60.7	60.1	60.2	60.6	60.7	—	—	60.6	60.7
1820–1830	61.1	61.2	61.2	61.2	61.0	61.1	—	—	—	—	—	—
1810–1820	61.5	61.6	61.5	61.6	61.5	61.6	—	—	—	—	—	—
1800–1810	61.8	61.8	61.8	61.8	61.8	61.8	—	—	—	—	—	—
1790–1800	62.0	62.0	—	—	—	—	—	—	—	—	—	—

t	*Missouri*		*North Dakota*		*South Dakota*		*Nebraska*		*Kansas*	
	Model 1	*Model 2*	*Model 1*	*Model 2*	*Model 1*	*Model 2*	*Model 1*	*Model 2*	*Model 1*	*Model 2*
1890–1900	40.5	51.2	36.9	54.1	23.2	50.4	29.6	50.7	43.0	52.6
1880–1890	47.0	53.8	45.2	55.9	34.0	53.5	39.3	53.6	48.7	54.8
1870–1880	51.5	55.9	50.6	57.3	42.7	55.9	46.7	56.0	52.5	56.5
1860–1870	54.9	57.5	54.7	58.5	50.3	57.8	52.5	57.7	55.5	57.9
1850–1860	57.9	58.8	58.2	59.4	56.7	59.0	57.3	58.9	58.2	59.1
1840–1850	59.7	59.9	—	—	—	—	—	—	—	—
1830–1840	60.6	60.7	—	—	—	—	—	—	—	—
1820–1830	61.2	61.3	—	—	—	—	—	—	—	—
1810–1820	61.5	61.6	—	—	—	—	—	—	—	—
1800–1810	—	—	—	—	—	—	—	—	—	—
1790–1800	—	—	—	—	—	—	—	—	—	—

Table VIA.5. Model 1 versus Model 3 Rural Crude Birth Rate Predictions for Each of the 23 Northern States, 1790–1800 to 1890–1900

	Maine		*New Hampshire*		*Vermont*		*Massachusetts*		*Rhode Island*		*Connecticut*	
t	*Model 1*	*Model 3*	*Model 1*	*Model 3*	*Model 1*	*Model 3*	*Model 1*	*Model 3*	*Model 1*	*Model 3*	*Model 1*	*Model 3*
1890–1900	22.3	22.0	22.3	22.0	22.3	22.0	22.3	22.0	22.3	22.0	22.3	22.0
1880–1890	25.0	23.4	25.0	23.4	25.0	23.4	25.0	23.4	25.0	23.4	25.0	23.4
1870–1880	27.4	26.2	27.4	26.2	27.4	26.2	27.4	26.2	27.4	26.2	27.4	26.2
1860–1870	29.9	29.1	29.9	29.1	29.9	29.1	29.9	29.1	29.9	29.1	29.9	29.1
1850–1860	33.3	32.7	33.0	32.7	33.0	32.7	33.0	32.7	33.0	32.7	33.0	32.7
1840–1850	41.7	41.5	35.4	35.3	35.4	35.3	35.4	35.3	35.4	35.3	35.4	35.3
1830–1840	47.3	47.2	36.9	36.9	38.5	38.1	36.9	36.9	36.9	36.9	36.9	36.9
1820–1830	51.6	51.6	38.0	38.0	45.7	45.5	38.0	38.0	38.0	38.0	38.0	38.0
1810–1820	54.8	54.8	42.7	42.7	51.2	51.2	38.7	38.7	38.7	38.7	39.1	39.1
1800–1810	57.0	57.0	47.6	47.6	54.4	54.4	43.7	43.7	39.3	39.3	44.5	44.5
1790–1800	58.6	58.6	51.6	51.6	56.7	56.7	48.4	48.4	44.1	44.1	49.1	49.1

	New York		*New Jersey*		*Pennsylvania*		*Delaware*		*Maryland*		*Ohio*	
t	*Model 1*	*Model 3*	*Model 1*	*Model 3*	*Model 1*	*Model 3*	*Model 1*	*Model 3*	*Model 1*	*Model 3*	*Model 1*	*Model 3*
1890–1900	22.3	22.0	22.3	22.0	22.3	22.0	22.3	22.0	22.3	22.0	22.3	22.0
1880–1890	25.0	23.4	25.0	23.4	25.0	23.4	25.0	23.4	25.0	23.4	25.0	23.4
1870–1880	27.4	26.2	27.4	26.2	27.4	26.2	27.4	26.2	27.4	26.2	27.4	26.2
1860–1870	29.9	29.1	29.9	29.1	30.2	29.1	29.9	29.1	29.9	29.1	34.9	32.9
1850–1860	33.0	32.7	33.0	32.7	38.5	37.9	33.0	32.7	33.0	32.7	45.2	44.4

1840–1850	37.5	37.3	35.4	35.3	45.5	45.3	35.4	35.3	35.4	35.3	54.6	54.4
1830–1840	47.9	47.8	38.1	37.9	50.4	50.3	36.9	36.9	36.9	36.9	58.9	58.8
1820–1830	53.0	52.9	44.3	44.2	54.0	54.0	38.0	38.0	38.6	38.6	61.1	61.1
1810–1820	56.2	56.2	49.3	49.3	56.5	56.5	41.3	41.3	44.1	44.1	61.5	61.5
1800–1810	58.2	58.2	52.9	52.9	58.2	58.2	46.4	46.4	48.7	48.7	61.8	61.8
1790–1800	59.6	59.6	55.6	55.6	59.5	59.5	50.6	50.6	52.4	52.4	62.0	62.0

	Indiana		*Illinois*		*Michigan*		*Wisconsin*		*Minnesota*		*Iowa*	
t	*Model 1*	*Model 3*	*Model 1*	*Model 3*	*Model 1*	*Model 3*	*Model 1*	*Model 3*	*Model 1*	*Model 3*	*Model 1*	*Model 3*
1890–1900	22.3	22.0	29.4	22.0	22.3	22.0	22.3	22.0	38.0	22.8	22.3	22.0
1880–1890	29.6	23.4	39.2	33.4	25.0	23.4	31.8	25.4	45.9	41.8	32.7	26.3
1870–1880	39.2	33.7	46.7	42.9	27.4	26.2	41.0	36.3	51.0	48.7	41.8	37.3
1860–1870	47.8	45.4	52.5	51.0	33.7	29.2	49.2	46.9	54.9	53.9	49.7	47.5
1850–1860	55.0	54.3	57.1	56.6	49.3	47.5	56.4	55.8	58.2	58.0	56.5	55.9
1840–1850	58.9	58.7	59.5	59.4	58.5	58.3	59.7	59.6	60.0	59.9	59.7	59.6
1830–1840	60.3	60.3	60.6	60.5	60.1	60.0	60.6	60.6	—	—	60.6	60.6
1820–1830	61.1	61.1	61.2	61.2	61.0	61.0	—	—	—	—	—	—
1810–1820	61.5	61.5	61.5	61.5	61.5	61.5	—	—	—	—	—	—
1800–1810	61.8	61.8	61.8	61.8	61.8	61.8	—	—	—	—	—	—
1790–1800	62.0	62.0	—	—	—	—	—	—	—	—	—	—

(*continued*)

Table VIA.5. (Continued)

	Missouri		*North Dakota*		*South Dakota*		*Nebraska*		*Kansas*	
t	*Model 1*	*Model 3*	*Model 1*	*Model 3*	*Model 1*	*Model 3*	*Model 1*	*Model 3*	*Model 1*	*Model 3*
1890–1900	40.5	33.6	36.9	22.0	23.2	22.0	29.6	22.0	43.0	33.8
1880–1890	47.0	43.5	45.2	40.9	34.0	27.7	39.3	33.8	48.7	45.6
1870–1880	51.5	49.4	50.6	48.1	42.7	38.5	46.7	43.2	52.5	50.7
1860–1870	54.9	54.0	54.7	53.6	50.3	48.3	52.5	51.0	55.5	54.7
1850–1860	57.9	57.6	58.2	57.9	56.7	56.2	57.3	56.8	58.2	57.9
1840–1850	59.7	59.6	—	—	—	—	—	—	—	—
1830–1840	60.6	60.6	—	—	—	—	—	—	—	—
1820–1830	61.2	61.2	—	—	—	—	—	—	—	—
1810–1820	61.5	61.5	—	—	—	—	—	—	—	—
1800–1810	—	—	—	—	—	—	—	—	—	—
1790–1800	—	—	—	—	—	—	—	—	—	—

Table VIA.6. Model 1 versus Model 4 Internal Density Predictions for Each of the 23 Northern States, 1790–1900

	Maine		*New Hampshire*		*Vermont*		*Massachusetts*		*Rhode Island*		*Connecticut*	
t	*Model 1*	*Model 4*	*Model 1*	*Model 4*	*Model 1*	*Model 4*	*Model 1*	*Model 4*	*Model 1*	*Model 4*	*Model 1*	*Model 4*
1900	—	—	—	—	—	—	—	—	—	—	—	—
1890	—	—	—	—	—	—	—	—	—	—	—	—
1880	—	—	—	—	—	—	—	—	—	—	—	—
1870	—	—	—	—	—	—	—	—	—	—	—	—
1860	1.00	—	—	—	—	—	—	—	—	—	—	—
1850	.99	—	—	—	—	—	—	—	—	—	—	—
1840	.78	1.00	—	—	1.00	—	—	—	—	—	—	—
1830	.61	.70	—	—	.94	1.00	—	—	—	—	—	—
1820	.46	.49	1.00	1.00	.71	.82	—	—	—	—	1.00	—
1810	.34	.35	.85	.88	.50	.52	1.00	1.00	—	—	.99	1.00
1800	.25	.25	.67	.67	.37	.37	.83	.83	1.00	1.00	.80	.80
1790	.18	.18	.52	.52	.28	.28	.66	.66	.83	.83	.63	.63

	New York		*New Jersey*		*Pennsylvania*		*Delaware*		*Maryland*		*Ohio*	
t	*Model 1*	*Model 4*	*Model 1*	*Model 4*	*Model 1*	*Model 4*	*Model 1*	*Model 4*	*Model 1*	*Model 4*	*Model 1*	*Model 4*
1900	—	—	—	—	—	—	—	—	—	—	—	—
1890	—	—	—	—	—	—	—	—	—	—	—	—
1880	—	—	—	—	—	—	—	—	—	—	—	—
1870	—	—	—	—	1.00	—	—	—	—	—	1.00	—
1860	—	—	—	—	.99	—	—	—	—	—	.84	1.00
1850	1.00	—	—	—	.82	1.00	—	—	—	—	.57	.85

(*continued*)

Table VIA.6. (Continued)

	New York		*New Jersey*		*Pennsylvania*		*Delaware*		*Maryland*		*Ohio*	
t	*Model 1*	*Model 4*	*Model 1*	*Model 4*	*Model 1*	*Model 4*	*Model 1*	*Model 4*	*Model 1*	*Model 4*	*Model 1*	*Model 4*
1840	.93	1.00	1.00	—	.63	.79	—	—	—	—	.26	.37
1830	.58	.67	.96	1.00	.48	.55	—	—	1.00	—	.10	.14
1820	.40	.43	.76	.84	.35	.38	1.00	1.00	.98	1.00	.01	.02
1810	.27	.28	.58	.60	.26	.26	.90	.94	.80	.82	.00	.00
1800	.19	.19	.44	.44	.19	.19	.72	.72	.63	.63	.00	.00
1790	.13	.13	.33	.33	.14	.14	.56	.56	.48	.48	.00	.00

	Indiana		*Illinois*		*Michigan*		*Wisconsin*		*Minnesota*		*Iowa*	
t	*Model 1*	*Model 4*	*Model 1*	*Model 4*	*Model 1*	*Model 4*	*Model 1*	*Model 4*	*Model 1*	*Model 4*	*Model 1*	*Model 4*
1900	—	—	.94	—	—	—	—	—	.72	—	—	—
1890	1.00	—	.79	—	—	—	1.00	—	.53	—	1.00	—
1880	.86	—	.56	—	—	—	.80	—	.33	—	.77	—
1870	.62	—	.36	1.00	1.00	—	.56	1.00	.20	1.00	.54	1.00
1860	.39	1.00	.20	.81	.88	1.00	.33	.95	.10	.35	.31	.90
1850	.18	.45	.09	.23	.41	.88	.12	.32	.03	.10	.11	.29
1840	.06	.16	.03	.08	.08	.25	.02	.07	.01	.02	.02	.07
1830	.02	.06	.01	.03	.03	.08	.01	.02	.00	.01	.01	.02
1820	.01	.02	.00	.01	.01	.02	.00	.01	.00	.00	.00	.01
1810	.00	.00	.00	.00	.00	.00	.00	.00	.00	.00	.00	.00
1800	.00	.00	.00	.00	.00	.00	.00	.00	.00	.00	.00	.00
1790	.00	.00	.00	.00	.00	.00	.00	.00	.00	.00	.00	.00

	Missouri		*North Dakota*		*South Dakota*		*Nebraska*		*Kansas*	
t	*Model 1*	*Model 4*	*Model 1*	*Model 4*	*Model 1*	*Model 4*	*Model 1*	*Model 4*	*Model 1*	*Model 4*
1900	.59	—	.78	—	1.00	—	.97	—	.49	—
1890	.44	—	.56	—	.97	—	.79	—	.36	—
1880	.29	—	.35	—	.73	—	.55	—	.23	—
1870	.18	1.00	.22	1.00	.50	1.00	.36	1.00	.14	1.00
1860	.10	.40	.11	.38	.29	.84	.20	.66	.08	.31
1850	.05	.13	.04	.11	.10	.27	.08	.20	.04	.10
1840	.02	.06	.01	.02	.02	.06	.02	.06	.02	.04
1830	.01	.02	.00	.01	.01	.02	.01	.02	.01	.02
1820	.00	.00	.00	.00	.00	.01	.00	.01	.00	.00
1810	.00	.00	.00	.00	.00	.00	.00	.00	.00	.00
1800	.00	.00	.00	.00	.00	.00	.00	.00	.00	.00
1790	.00	.00	.00	.00	.00	.00	.00	.00	.00	.00

NOTES AND REFERENCES

1. The outline for this model was suggested by Richard A. Easterlin, "A Model of Rural Population Growth in the American North," paper presented at the Landon Project Symposium, "A Blueprint for Interdisciplinary Regional History," University of Western Ontario, September, 1977, who, in discussing the buildup of the rural population of the United States, had proposed a method for simulating the U.S. experience. In that exercise, destination states for out-migration as well as fertility rates were given exogenously.

2. European immigration is allocated to New York where it is eventually distributed to other parts of the region. This flow begins during the 1790–1800 decade and continues throughout the period. Specifically, the number of European immigrants is multiplied by the percentage of the population in New York residing in rural areas to produce estimates of the number of European immigrants going to rural New York. These estimates are as follows: 32,100 for 1790–1800; 18,700 for 1800–1810; 46,600 for 1810–1820; 87,674 for 1820–1830; 359,785 for 1830–1840; 1,103,659 for 1840–1850; 1,880,998 for 1850–1860; 1,139,857 for 1860–1870; 1,126,099 for 1870–1880; 2,023,065 for 1880–1890 and 1,249,405 for 1890–1900. After rural New York is completely settled (about 1850), these people are redistributed to rural areas of states with available land after multiplying by the percentage rural in the region. For example, by 1890–1900, 80.6% of the European immigrants are allocated to urban areas ((1 − (.349)(.555)), where the percent rural equals .349 and .555 in New York and in the entire region, respectively). Migration from the southern states is allocated to Ohio where it is eventually distributed to other mid-western states. The percent rural in Ohio is used to allocate the southern migration between rural and urban areas. This flow begins during the 1820–1830 decade with 120,213 migrants, continues with 176,283 for 1830–1840 and 288,914 for 1840–1850, and ends with 106,768 in 1850–1860. These estimates were derived from data found in Larry Neal and Paul Uselding, "Immigration, A Neglected Source of American Economic Growth: 1790 to 1812," *Oxford Economic Papers,* 2nd Series, Vol. 24, March, 1972, 68–88, and U.S. Bureau of the Census, *Seventh Census of the United States: 1850* (Washington, D.C., 1853), *U.S. Census of Population: 1960, Vol. I, Characteristics of the Population, Part I, United States Summary* (Washington, D.C., 1964), and *Historical Statistics of the United States, Colonial Times to 1957* (Washington, D.C., 1960). It is assumed that these migrants enter at a uniform rate throughout each decade and, therefore, their rate of natural increase during the initial decade of migration is one half of the rate applied to individuals who spend the entire decade in the state.

3. While, in reality, out-migration began before a state reached its maximum rural population, Easterlin, "Population Change," estimates that *net* out-migration usually began within a short time before 90% of the maximum population had been reached. For example, net out-migration apparently began around three years before Illinois and Nebraska were 90% settled. The

earliest net out-migration, for New Hampshire, began twenty years before the 90% settlement figure was reached.

4. See Morton Owen Schapiro, "Internal Migration in the United States: Evidence From the Early 19th Century" (April 1982), for the estimation of a variant of this equation which differentiates between push and pull factors and between the relative attractiveness of rural and urban areas.

5. The only time the actual values of the internal and total density measures are used is for the decade 1790–1800. Predicted values are used during all other decades.

6. As discussed in Section III.2, fertility model predictions using actual density values appear to be too low at the end of the period. This helps explain why Model 1 underestimates rural population growth.

7. State-specific rural crude birth rate predictions from Model 1 are presented in Section VI.5, Table VIA.1.

8. These empirical results are generally consistent with Easterlin's "Population Change" findings.

9. These crude birth rates are as follows: Maine: 58.6, New Hampshire: 51.6, Vermont: 56.7, Massachusetts: 48.4, Rhode Island: 44.1, Connecticut: 49.1, New York: 59.6, New Jersey: 55.6, Pennsylvania: 59.5, Delaware: 50.6, Maryland: 52.4, Ohio: 58.9, Indiana: 58.9, Illinois: 57.1, Michigan: 58.5, Wisconsin: 59.7, Minnesota: 58.2, Iowa: 59.7, Missouri: 57.9, North Dakota: 58.2, South Dakota: 59.7, Nebraska: 57.3, and Kansas: 55.5.

10. State-specific internal density predictions from Model 2 are presented in Section VI.5, Table VIA.2.

11. State-specific internal density predictions from Model 3 are presented in Section VI.5, Table VIA.3.

12. This result supports Francis Walker's hypothesis that immigration led to a reduction in native fertility. See Francis A. Walker, "Immigration and Degradation," *The Forum,* 11 (Aug. 1891). State-specific rural crude birth rate predictions from Model 2 are presented in Section VI.5, Table VIA.4. When European immigration during the 1790–1900 period is ignored, the northern rural population is directly reduced by about 9 million people (the sum of the immigration estimates) and is reduced further by removing the descendents of European immigrants. However, the fertility response is large enough to lower the net population effect to a loss of under 7 million people.

13. State-specific rural crude birth rate predictions from Model 3 are presented in Section VI.5, Table VIA.5.

14. State-specific internal density predictions from Model 4 are presented in Section VI.5, Table VIA.6.

15. Since the entire area would have been settled, the program was terminated.

16. Turner, "The Significance."

17. Dov Friedlander, "Demographic Responses and Population Change," *Demography,* 6 (Nov. 1969), 359–381, argues that industrialization provides the opportunity for rural-urban migration, reducing rural pressure for fertility reduction. In a more recent article, "Demographic Responses and So-

cioeconomic Structure: Population Processes in England and Wales in the Nineteenth Century," *Demography*, 20 (Aug. 1983), 249–272, he examined a group of 600 geographical units in England and Wales during the period 1851–1910 and found that emigration and a decline in marital fertility were substitute responses in agricultural-based districts. The notion that population pressure may precipitate a variety of demographic responses was explored earlier in Kingsley Davis, "The Theory of Change and Response in Modern Demographic History," *Population Index*, 29 (Oct. 1963), 345–366.

Chapter VII

Implications for the Developing World

The theoretical and empirical analysis of nineteenth century U.S. population growth and distribution has been completed. In this chapter, the principal conclusions are outlined (VII.1), the situation in today's developing countries is discussed and lessons from the experience of the historical United States are applied (VII.2), and, finally, some general conclusions are presented (VII.3).

VII.1 CONCLUSIONS FROM THE U.S. ANALYSIS

Several prominent implications can be drawn from the partial equilibrium analyses of fertility and migration and from the general dynamic analysis of the settlement process. These conclusions are broken down by type and topic of analysis with the fertility [F] results based on Chapters II and III, the migration [M] results based on Chapters IV and V and the settlement [S] results based on Chapter VI.

[F1] A prominent feature of U.S. demographic history was the decline in birth rates in rural areas of the northern states.

The rural decline in birth rates is shown vividly in Table III.3 which contains a panel of crude birth rate predictions for the

23 states during the period lasting from 1790–1800 to 1890–1900. By the midpoint in this period (1840–1850) the weighted average of the crude birth rate estimates had fallen by 18.7%, from 54.1 to 44.0. By the end of the century the average had fallen an additional 45.9% to 23.8. While the final few crude birth rate estimates appear to be too low (these estimates imply a 56.0% decline over the entire period), it is reasonable to conclude that the decline in rural birth rates in the northern states was in the order of 50% by the end of the century. Thus, birth rates were reduced by roughly half during the ten decades after the decade 1790–1800.

[F2] The probable explanation for the decline in birth rates was a decrease in the demand for children.

Section II.2 applied a general theoretical model of fertility determination to the historical experience of the United States. It was shown that a decline in the number of surviving children could result from a decline in the natural supply (possibly due to an increase in mortality rates) if the U.S. were in an excess demand situation (Stage I). Instead, if an excess supply situation prevailed (Stage II or III), either an increase in the natural supply, a decrease in the costs of fertility regulation or a decrease in the demand for children could be responsible for the decline in fertility rates. Since mortality conditions were apparently stable and there was no significant change in fertility regulation costs, a decline in the demand for children was the likely factor leading to the observed reduction in birth rates. Perhaps the most important conclusion is not simply that the demand for children fell but that neither a decrease in mortality rates nor an increase in the availability of contraceptives were necessary conditions for a reduction in fertility rates.

[F3] The decrease in the demand for children was associated with a growing scarcity of land.

The discussion of [F2] raises the question of why the United States violated the normal pattern of the demographic transition by having a widespread decline in fertility almost a century before any lasting improvement in mortality conditions. The empirical analysis demonstrated that the principal components of the crude birth rate—the birth ratio and the proportion of reproductive females—were closely tied to variations in the availability of farmland (Tables III.1 and III.2). Since this result was generated using panel data and an error components generalized least-squares regression procedure, it can be concluded that land availability was a critical factor in explaining movements in fertility rates across states and over time.

[F4] A plausible explanation for the success of the land availability measures is that changes in the availability of land affect the ability to provide for children in the desired manner.

Section II.2 discussed possible explantions for the ability of land availability variables to explain variations in birth rates at various levels of aggregation. As land becomes more scarce, the numerator of a relative income variable may fall, reflecting a decline in prospective income. Specifically, for a variety of reasons, farmers in older, more settled areas sometimes experienced a tighter budget constraint (due, for example, to a decline in the arability of land resulting from its overuse), while, at the same time, population pressures increased the price of land, thereby making it harder for young couples to establish farms of their own. The resulting combination of lower marital fertility and an increase in the average age at first marriage led to lower birth rates. The association between the availability of land and fertility is strengthened by movements in aspiration income. The amount of resources parents need before having some number of children depends on social attitudes concerning the intergenerational transfer of wealth. When there is a strong bequest motive in which parents seek to provide farmland for children which maintains some minimum efficient size, the decrease in farm profitability and/or the increase in the price of new land would reduce the ability of parents to satisfy their bequest goals. Thus, the decline in land availability may make it more difficult to provide for children in the desired manner and the corresponding decrease in birth rates may reflect the attempt not to exceed the optimal number of heirs. If, on the other hand, parents had not been concerned with maintaining some minimum efficient farm size, the relationship between land availability and birth rates would have been weaker as parents would simply divide their farmland among their children.

[F5] People responded to changes in the environment both by delaying marriage and by reducing marital fertility.

In his classic piece on population, Malthus predicted that high rates of population growth would continue as long as productive land generated a food supply sufficient to satisfy the needs of the population.[1] In fact, he cited the United States case as a prime example of circumstances leading to extremely rapid, perhaps unparalleled, population growth. However, Malthus believed that it was inevitable that eventually the growth in population would create severe strains on food production, at which point the rate of population increase would decline. Specifically, while some preventive checks such as an increase in the marriage age would take place, the dominant factor reducing population growth would be an increase in mortality as a growing number of people are reduced to subsistence standards of living, thereby becoming vulnerable to even minor shortfalls in food production.

The key assumption of a simple Malthusian model is that preventive checks are relatively unimportant—"that the passion between the sexes is necessary and will remain nearly in its present state," thereby dominating human behavior.[2] Thus, changes in marital customs and marital fertility would not significantly slow the growth of population. Instead, the positive check of higher mortality would eventually bring the population into balance with available resources.

This hypothesis is not consistent with the preceding analysis. Malthus was correct in stating that the United States had a great deal of available land at the end of the eighteenth century and, correspondingly, had extremely high birth rates. However, when land became increasingly scarce, not only did marital customs change (the average age at first marriage increased and the proportion married fell) but, more significantly, marital fertility decreased as well. As described in Section III.4 (and later in Section VI.4), the decline in birth rates acted as a safety valve which prevented the horrors that Malthus had envisioned. The case of the historical United States clearly demonstrates that rational individuals do in fact react to changes in the environment. When preventive checks are strong, there need not be an increase in mortality in order to regulate population growth.

[M1] The availability of land was an important factor in allocating the migration stream among destination states.

The estimation results presented in Table V.1 show that, all things equal, migrants were more likely to settle in a state which contained available land than in a state characterized by land scarcity. This finding is consistent with Turner's view that cheap, productive land in the West served as a powerful attraction to Eastern farmers trying to support their families on their relatively expensive, less productive land.[3]

[M2] The selection of destination states was also affected by distance, regional affinity, and the desire to move to the west.

Table V.1 shows that migrants sought to minimize the distance traveled, favored remaining on roughly the same latitude, and preferred available land in the west over available land in the east.

[M3] The behavior of migrants selecting destination states can be accounted for by factors which are consistent with the human capital approach.

As explained in Section IV.1, the human capital approach applies the neoclassical theory of investment to the migration decision. Rational economic behavior is assumed as migrants, in the manner of other investors, maximize the present value of the future earnings stream net of costs. Here, the benefits from migration are measured by the increase in the ability to purchase productive farmland and the fact that a destination state is in the expanding and developing West while the costs are measured by distances and regional dissimilarities. In sum, [M1] and [M2] imply that the behavior of the migration stream during the first half of the nineteenth century was influenced by changes in the environment which resulted in a logical response consistent with economic theory.

[S1] The pattern of settlement in the nineteenth century United States was in large part determined by the effects of declining land availability on fertility and migration.

The control solution analyzed in Section VI.2 demonstrates that the availability of land was the key to explaining the general pattern of slow population growth, followed by rapid growth, which eventually leveled off at some stable level. When land was easily available, in-migration accounted for most of the growth in population, since high birth rates had a limited effect given the small population base. However, as this base grew, the high rate of natural increase along with continued in-migration led to a rapid increase in the population. Eventually, however, land became scarce, birth rates fell, and, as the state became less attractive to migrants seeking a destination state, in-migration fell as well. A stable population is achieved when there is no available land and out-migration reallocates the excess population (resulting from a relatively small but positive rate of natural increase) to cities and to states with available land. This result, along with [F5] and [M3], demonstrates once again that the eventual leveling off of the rural population was a rational response to changes in the environment. Rural population pressures were dissipated by out-migration (rural-rural and rural-urban) and by the rural fertility decline. These safety valves were successful in replacing Malthus' ultimate population check—an increase in mortality. In sum, there were three safety valves as individuals reacted rationally to the growing scarcity of land in the following manner:

1. by moving to the frontier;
2. by moving to cities; and
3. by reducing their demand for children, and, ultimately, the birth rate.

These factors, rather than mortality, brought rural population growth to a halt.

[S2] The strains of population growth result in a multiple, interrelated response.

The analysis in Chapter VI strongly suggests that trade-offs exist among the different safety valves. Model 3 showed that, if the rural-urban option were removed, fertility rates would have been lower. However, since the decline in the rate of natural increase would have only partially mediated the effects of no rural to urban migration, rural population pressures would have increased, resulting in higher rates of rural-rural migration and an increase in the settlement rate of the region. If rural fertility had not reacted to increasing land scarcity, the results from Model 4 show an increase in rural-urban migration and a much larger absolute increase in rural-rural migration, leading to the significantly faster settlement of the rural north. Other scenarios could have also been explored. For example, what if there had been no frontier (i.e., no available land)? Again, the multiple responses of more rural-urban migration and a larger decline in rural fertility would have mediated against the creation of unmanageable population pressure manifested in a deterioration in rural living standards, a susceptibility to shortfalls in food production, and the resulting increase in mortality.

It is apparent that a general dynamic approach is needed in order to explain population growth and distribution. The possibility of multiple responses is ignored in partial equilibrium analyses in which fertility is examined while migration is assumed to be exogenous or migration is examined with fertility treated as exogenous. In reality, fertility and migration react to similar factors and are critically intertwined. In the case of the historical United States, a model in which fertility, migration and population growth could be examined simultaneously was essential in explaining the settlement pattern.

VII.2 RELEVANCE FOR THE DEVELOPING WORLD

It is widely believed that population problems have hindered economic growth in developing countries. For several decades, government planners have attempted to solve these problems through a variety of programs and policies, and, while there have been successes, the results have frequently been disappointing.

The most prominent problem is the extremely high rates of natural increase experienced in many countries throughout the developing world. Since World War II, there have been notable advances in health and nutrition which have led to improvements in mortality levels. While this is certainly a "giant step forward for humanity," it creates some important costs in the form of rapid population growth which may hamper increases in per capita income. Planners believe that facilitating a decline in fertility rates would promote economic growth, and well over one hundred governments officially support programs with that aim.[4]

Yet, despite government concerns and the allocation of extremely scarce resources toward the goal of reducing fertility levels, population growth in many developing countries has remained at very high levels.[5] Why have government programs met with only limited success? The answer to this question may be found by returning to the general fertility model described above (Section II.1).

At an early stage of development, an excess demand for surviving children may exist. The price of children is low since the direct costs of supporting children (food, clothing and shelter) tend to be relatively small in a typical rural environment. In addition, the absence of a strong negative link between number of children and female labor force participation means that the indirect cost of children (the opportunity cost of a woman's time) will also be low, while limited exposure to market goods maintains low material aspirations and strong preferences for children as the main source of parents' utility. Finally, and perhaps most importantly, children are a source of present and future income and a "social security effect" exists, also leading to a high demand for children. Since high infant and child mortality rates introduce considerable uncertainty into reaching the desired number of surviving children, risk averse parents may opt for substantially more births than their number of desired children in order to avoid the unfortunate consequences which accompany child mortality after the age at which replacement becomes impossible. This "insurance effect" implies that a high demand for surviving children is associated with an even higher optimal number of births. On the other hand, the natural supply is limited by health and nutrition constraints as well as by social mores concerning such important factors as lactation (which increases the length of the average birth interval). In total, the desired number of births exceeds the number of births which occur when no effort is made to restrict fertility and the resulting birth rate is constrained by natural fertility factors.[6] As the development process progresses, the desired number of surviving children decreases, mortality rates fall, and, therefore, the desired number of births falls. The natural supply of births increases and eventually surpasses the demand. However, fertility regulation does not take place until the disutility associated with unregulated fertility exceeds the disutility accompanying fertility regulation.

The basic assumption of population programs in most developing countries has been that there is an unfilled need for fertility regulation information and devices.[7] The idea that birth rates would fall if fertility regulation costs were lowered has been the maintained hypothesis underlying many of these fertility control programs. However, the general fertility model shows that an excess demand for births rather than an excess supply may be the case in parts of the developing world. If this is so, when the social security, insurance and other effects produce a situation in which people seek to increase or maintain rather than decrease birth rates, this type of population program has no chance for success. Even when an excess supply situation is present, the disutility associated with unwanted births may be quite small and, again, the returns to increasing contraceptive accessibility would be minimal.

Lowering the cost of fertility regulation is an easier, more certain task than lowering the demand for surviving children or for births, and this may explain why planners have favored this approach. However, it is clear that a revolution in contraceptive availability is not a sufficient condition for lowering the rate of natural increase.[8] Is it a necessary condition?

The conclusions based on the analysis of the U.S. experience offer considerable insight into the successes and failures of population programs in the developing world. [F2] stated that birth rates fell as the demand for children decreased, despite little change in fertility regulation costs. Thus, for the United States, increases in contraceptive availability were not a necessary condition for lowering birth rates. The paradox is that birth rates in many developing countries remain stable despite reductions in regulation costs while birth rates in the United States fell while regulation costs remained unchanged. The explanation is simple: the United States was in an excess supply situation and a decline in the demand for children increased the disutility associated with unregulated fertility to the point where it exceeded the costs of fertility regulation. Hence, while a reduction in regulation costs presumably would have led to an even faster decrease in birth rates, it was not needed to induce people to start regulating their fertility. On the other hand, efforts aimed at reducing regulation costs are superfluous in the excess demand situation experienced in some developing countries.

This is not to say that the U.S. experience implies that planners should never allocate resources to reducing regulation costs. The discussion of [F1] showed that it took a century for fertility rates to decline by one half.[9] The developing world may not be able to afford that much time and, where an excess supply situation exists, reducing regulation costs should facilitate the decline in birth rates.

Another implication of [F2] is that reductions in mortality rates are not a necessary condition for lowering birth rates, directly refuting the theory of the demographic transition. However, while mortality conditions may have been stable in the nineteenth century United States, mortality rates were quite low compared to the rest of the world at the time. Had mortality been higher, then it is unlikely that the demand for children would have fallen enough to have created an excess supply situation and the eventual reduction in birth rates which accompanied the regulation of fertility. Recent advances have lowered mortality rates in most developing countries far below levels in the historical United States and additional reductions should have the same effect that the reduction in the demand for children had in the United States—a fall in birth rates as the disutility associated with unregulated fertility increases. In sum, further reductions in mortality in developing countries could help change an excess demand situation to one of excess supply, or, if an excess supply situation already prevails, a decline in mortality could induce people to regulate their fertility. While mortality and regulation cost reductions were not necessary conditions for a birth rate decrease in the United States, that is because an excess supply situation already existed and a decline in the demand for children was sufficient. However, in the developing world, a decline in mortality rates could be an important factor leading to the eventual usefulness of a program aimed at increasing contraceptive knowledge and availability.

[F3] states that the critical causal factor in the U.S. fertility decline, the reduction in the demand for children, was associated with a decline in the availability of land. Can we expect this to be the case in the developing world as well? If an excess demand situation exists then it is possible that land scarcity would lower the demand for children enough that it would be below the natural supply, creating some motivation for fertility regulation. If an excess supply situation already exists, then the disutility associated with unregulated fertility would become even greater as land became more scarce. Therefore, population planners could have a windfall in that birth rates may fall independently of any population program.

In order to determine the likelihood of an automatic reduction in birth rates accompanying growing land scarcity, [F4] must be examined. A plausible reason that the demand for children fell as land became more scarce is that the ratio of prospective to minimum income fell. Of particular importance was the role that bequest aspirations played as a component of minimum income. Increasing land scarcity in the United States meant the growing inability of parents to provide farmland for their children without fragmenting farms below some minimum efficient size. Without this bequest motive, land scarcity may still imply a tighter budget constraint and a reduction in the consumption of all normal goods including children, but this is unlikely to be very important in most developing countries where the costs of children are very low or even negative (if the social security effect is strong enough). Thus, unless parents in developing countries feel obligated to transfer wealth to their children without breaking up the family farm into units insufficiently large to be economically viable, the link between land availability, the demand for children, and birth rates will be weakened.

The formation of social mores concerning intergenerational wealth transfer is an important issue. In some areas, farm fragmentation continued far below efficient levels and agricultural production suffered greatly. Why was the northern United States apparently different?[10] Possibly the background of the early colonists affected their aspirations and the aspirations of their descendents. More likely, the nature of U.S. development—the growth of cities, for example—may have created sufficient non-farm opportunities for children that parents were able to provide for their children without the transfer of farmland. Greven, for example, found that as land became more scarce in Massachusetts, it became increasingly popular for parents to pay for their children's education and to establish them in trades.[11] In many developing countries, where these non-farm opportunities are rarer, it is less likely that a bequest motive maintaining efficient farm size will last. In sum, the unexpected windfall of an automatic reduction in birth rates as land becomes scarce may very well occur in some developing countries but it is possible that the case of the United States was exceptional in the strength of the land availability-demand for children relationship.[12]

How does the most critical fertility conclusion, [F5]—that people react rationally to changes in the environment—relate to the developing world? In the United States, the change in marital customs and marital fertility prevented the buildup of excessive population pressures. Yet in the developing world, Malthus' prediction that the lack of preventive checks would drive the population to subsistence levels, increasing their susceptibility to shortfalls in food production, seems to have some validity. However, what was rational for a farmer in the rural northern United States may not be rational for an individual in one of today's developing countries. Factors mentioned above such as the social security effect, the insurance effect, isolation from markets, low opportunity costs associated with child rearing, and, possibly, the lack of a bequest motive maintaining minimum farm size, lead to high demand for children in developing countries, and, even when standards of living are low, there may be little or no incentive to regulate fertility.[13] Thus, rapid population growth continues but not because passion reigns over intellect. Rather, economic and social factors are responsible for the demand for large families and the reluctance to engage in fertility regulation (or to delay marriage) is, itself, a rational response. Will people ultimately breed themselves to death? It should be remembered that mortality rates have in fact changed significantly during the past several decades but that this change has been in the direction of an improvement—not a deterioration—in mortality conditions. If population pressures begin to reverse the mortality trend, then rational individuals will again weigh the relevant costs and benefits and, presumably, they will restrict their fertility.[14] Rather than wait for this to occur, population planners should follow the emerging consensus that the best way to lower fertility is by changing the institutions, mores and economic factors which cause people to desire a large number of children.[15] Providing old age security, increasing exposure to market goods and increasing female labor force participation rates and educational levels are ways to induce a decline in the demand for children. In the United States these changes happened without any intentional government actions. In the developing world, planners can and should facilitate these changes in order to hasten the demographic transition. These policies may not be as straightforward as providing contraceptives, but the results are likely to be far more impressive.

Population problems in developing countries are not limited

to concern about high birth rates. Much attention has been paid to migration problems, in particular, excessive rural to urban migration.

In many countries, rural migrants have been attracted by the prospects of urban life and have left rural areas in disturbing numbers.[16] The results have been twofold: (1) food production in rural areas has been adversely affected by out-migration, especially since the migration stream has been weighted in terms of young males; and (2) urban areas have expanded more rapidly than employment opportunities, creating a large class of "underground" or sub-employed workers. Why then do migrants continue to move from rural to urban areas? The low probability of primary sector urban employment is offset by the high earnings accompanying such employment, causing the expected value of urban earnings to exceed the expected value of rural earnings (where the high probability of employment is offset by low wages).[17] The favored policy prescriptions, therefore, are to encourage rural investment (thereby increasing rural wages), to provide greater amenities in rural areas (for example, schools and hospitals) and, in general, to make rural areas more attractive.

[M1] showed that, in the United States, an important factor determining the attractiveness of an area was the availability of cheap, productive farmland. It is reasonable to expect that in developing countries, growing land scarcity will encourage even greater rural out-migration, compounding the migration problem.[18] [M2] implies that the destination of out-migrants depends on other factors as well. All of the factors, as explained in the discussion of [M3], are consistent with the belief that migrants weigh the costs and benefits of out- and in-migration and behave in the manner of any other rational investor. Clearly, migration policies along the lines of those mentioned above could result in the desired outcome. By changing the values of the relevant economic variables, the magnitude and direction of the migration stream can be altered. Yet, in the United States, migration was a response to high wages, and in the words of Kuznets:

> Since economic growth is measured primarily as an increase in output, and since internal migration toward greater earning opportunities is

> also migration toward greater production opportunities, such internal migration is partly responsible for economic growth: without it some of the economic growth that was realized would not have been possible.[19]

Why then should planners in developing countries interfere with the market? The answer lies in the expected income analysis presented above. Individuals migrate to cities, not because good economic opportunities await, but because some people earn very high incomes (relative to the alternatives). There is limited access to high primary sector earnings; nevertheless, these wages attract migrants who become part of the extremely high unemployment. Thus, the stratification of the markets allows primary sector wages to remain high even as the supply of secondary workers increases. It is clear that the market mechanism does not lead to the best allocation of labor resources and planners are forced to interfere with market forces in order to pursue their development goals. Moreover, previous interference by planners quite probably exacerbated the rural-urban migration problem as pro-urbanization and industrialization policies increased the expected value of urban earnings. Thus, alternative policies may merely lessen the adverse effects of prior government actions.

Finally, the conclusions from the settlement analysis can be applied. [S1] addressed the Malthusian belief that only mortality increases can ultimately reduce population pressure by presenting three alternative safety valves. As discussed above, if these automatic reactions to increasing land scarcity do in fact occur in developing countries, it will have a beneficial effect on a program aimed at reducing population growth rates and a negative effect on a program aimed at stemming the tide of rural-urban migration. However, when the two are examined together, the long-run migration effect may be favorable as lower rural fertility now implies less out-migration later. Thus, the short-run effect may worsen the urban migration problem but eventually the severity of the problem should be reduced.

This sort of interrelationship relates to the second settlement conclusion, [S2], that there are multiple, interrelated responses to population pressure. Links between fertility and migration must be recognized by planners in order to avoid unintended adverse consequences of their programs. For instance, as mentioned above, proposed ways to reduce excessive rural-urban migration have included making rural areas more attractive places to live by increasing amenities and stimulating rural investment. However, the settlement analysis suggests that policies aimed at reducing rural out-migration may, in fact, inhibit reductions in rural fertility. For example, if rural investment increased family income, the demand for children (all else being equal) will rise, not only frustrating those planners concerned with reducing already high rates of natural increase but also creating additional out-migration pressure a generation later.[20] Clearly, government attempts at improving rural conditions should not only reduce rural-urban migration but, at the same time, should facilitate the reduction in rural fertility. An example of such a policy would be to create female non-farm employment opportunities, thereby making rural areas more attractive while raising the indirect cost of children and reducing birth rates. On the other hand, stressing urbanization as a development goal would not only encourage rural-urban migration but the effect of this migration would be to dissipate population pressure in rural areas, thereby slowing the rate of rural fertility decline and possibly leading to even greater rural-urban migration at a later date.

It should be clear that the interrelated nature of fertility and migration behavior could cause planners concerned only with partial equilibrium effects to implement policies which have severe, unexpected consequences. While the strength of these interrelationships will certainly vary across countries, they must be studied in order to provide information from which the most effective policies can be based. Relying on the results from partial equilibrium analyses to formulate population policy may create as many problems as it solves. A general dynamic analysis, on the other hand, can be used to, at best, solve several problems at once or, at worst, to minimize any secondary problems which may be created.

VII.3 CONCLUSION

The goal of this study has been to gain insight into the factors which affected the complicated picture of population growth and distribution in the nineteenth-century United States. By relying on both partial equilibrium and general dynamic approaches, a variety of specific and more general questions were addressed, and a set of conclusions were produced which not only represent a more detailed understanding of U.S. demographic history but also have some potentially important implications for population programs in today's developing world.

Yet, this is certainly not the final word concerning the settlement of the United States. The historical experience of the United States represents a valuable source of information which should be exploited. For instance, future research could expand the present study in a number of ways: the model could be expanded to incorporate data from all of the states; both urbanization and immigration could be endogenously determined within the model; land availability could be linked more concretely to economic variables and the predicted values of these variables could serve as independent variables in the fertility and migration sub-models; attempts could be made to more clearly distinguish between the effects of changes in marital customs and changes in marital fertility; the link between land scarcity, input use and technological change could be examined in an analysis of how maximum populations are determined and how they can be changed; and less aggregated data could be used in estimating several of the key equations. Of course, these extensions are limited by the severe lack of data in almost all areas of U.S. demographic history. As these gaps are filled, a more sophisticated settlement model can be specified and estimated which more realistically mirrors the U.S. experience. In any case, the form of the settlement model, with its largely closed general dynamic structure, facilitates the examination of questions which are beyond the scope of a more limited analysis.

While economists, demographers and historians have long speculated about the factors which underlie the pattern of rural settlement in the historical United States, little has been done to empirically evaluate their hypotheses. The present study has sought to push forward the debate by using a new methodology and asking a number of questions of broad importance. It is hoped that these findings and methods will stimulate additional research in the area of U.S. demographic history—an area in which much work remains to be done.

NOTES AND REFERENCES

1. Thomas Robert Malthus, *An Essay on the Principles of Population,* originally published in 1789, reprinted (England, 1979).
2. Malthus, *An Essay,* p. 70.
3. See his quote in Section III.4.
4. See "Family Planning in the 1980's: Challenges and Opportunities," Recommendations of the International Conference on Family Planning in the 1980s, Jakarta, Indonesia, April 26–30, 1981, *Studies in Family Planning,* 12 (June/July 1981), 251–256. For a review of the literature concerning the positive and negative links between population and economic growth see Geoffrey McNicoll, "Consequences of Rapid Population Growth: An Overview and Assessment," *Population and Development Review,* 10 (June 1984), 177–240.
5. Figures from the *World Development Report 1984,* (Oxford, 1984), show that the average annual population growth rate for low-income nations other than China and India equaled 2.6% from 1970–1980 with a predicted value for 1980–2000 of 2.9%. The comparable figures for the lower middle-income nations are 2.5% for 1970–1980 and 2.4% for 1980–2000. These numbers can be contrasted with .7% and .4% for the industrial market nations.
6. See Figure II.1 for a picture of the stages of fertility determination in which the number of surviving children rather than the number of births is examined. The major analytical difference between the two is that mortality enters the demand function for births and the supply function for surviving children. The conclusions regarding the potential for fertility regulation are the same in either case.
7. For a review of population policies in eight developing countries, see Donald P. Warwick, *Bitter Pills* (Cambridge, 1982).
8. See, for example, Thomas E. Dow, Jr. and Linda H. Werner, "Family Size and Family Planning in Kenya," *Studies in Family Planning,* 12 (June/July 1981), 272–277, and Robert Cuca and Catherine S. Pierce, *Experiments in Family Planning* (Baltimore, 1977). There are many other examples where family planning methods are approved of and available but are nonetheless used only to a limited extent. Thomas Dow, "Fertility and Family Planning in Sierra Leone," *Studies in Family Planning,* 2 (May 1971), 153–165, presents data showing that 74% of the women interviewed had specific knowledge of family planning methods, 65% approved of family planning, but only 18% had ever practiced family planning. Nasra M. Shah, "Past and Current Contraceptive Use in Pakistan," *Studies in Family Planning,* 10 (May 1979), 164–173, found that while about 80% of married women surveyed knew of a modern method of fertility control and over 60% knew of the birth control pill, fewer than 10% of these women used any of these methods and less than 4% used the pill. As indicated by Warwick, *Bitter Pills,* it has been clear since 1970 that, in many countries, the supply of family planning services has greatly exceeded the demand.

9. [F1] also showed that urbanization-industrialization was not a necessary condition for reducing birth rates, thereby challenging another contention of many of today's population programs.

10. Gary D. Libecap and George Alter, "Agricultural Productivity, Partible Inheritance, and the Demographic Response to Rural Poverty: An Examination of the Spanish Southwest," *Explorations in Economic History,* 19 (April 1982), 184–200, found that a partible inheritance system in Hispanic New Mexico resulted in inefficiently small farms and rural poverty. On the other hand, in his study of Andover, Massachusetts, Greven, *Four Generations,* found that parents were extremely reluctant to divide their farms below a minimum level of about thirty acres.

11. Greven, *Four Generations.* At the same time, birth rates fell as marital customs changed (the average age at first marriage rose) and marital fertility fell.

12. Glenn Firebaugh, "Population Density and Fertility in 22 Indian Villages," *Demography,* 19 (Nov. 1982), 481–494, found that rural fertility in India fell as land became more scarce. Further, in a study of the fertility decline in Thailand, John Knodel, Napaporn Havanon and Anthony Pramualratana, "A Tale of Two Generations: A Qualitative Analysis of Fertility Transition in Thailand," *Population and Development Review,* 10 (June 1984), 297–328, it was discovered that the growing inability to provide farmland for children without what was perceived as excessive fragmentation resulted in attempts not only to educate children in order to increase their chances for nonagricultural employment but also to reduce family size. Whether the land availability-fertility link is present in other developing countries is an interesting and important question for further study. In any case, the presence of an automatic fertility decline in India and Thailand should be encouraging news to population planners.

13. This does not necessarily mean that society is made better off by large families. As argued by E. A. Wrigley, "Fertility Strategy for the Individual and the Group," in *Historical Studies,* Tilley, ed., rational individuals may act in a way which is counter to the interests of society.

14. For example, food scarcity would result in higher prices, thereby raising the direct cost of children and lowering demand.

15. For an excellent collection of papers concerning fertility (several of which have been cited above) see *Historical Studies,* Tilly, ed. Tilly's two papers in this volume, "The Historical Study of Vital Processes," and "Questions and Conclusions," relate to a number of issues discussed in Chapter VII.

16. See, for example, Dipak Mazumdar, *The Urban Labor Market and Income Distribution: A Study of Malaysia* (World Bank, 1981), Arthur Silvers and Pierre Crosson, *Rural Development and Urban-Bound Migration in Mexico* (Resources for the Future, 1980), and Michael Lipton, "Migration from Rural Areas of Poor Countries: The Impact on Rural Productivity and Income Distribution," *World Development,* 8 (No. 1, 1980), 1–24.

17. See Michael P. Todaro, "A Model of Labor Migration and Urban Unemployment in Less Developed Countries," *American Economic Review,* 59 (March 1969), 138–148.

18. This was found to be the case by Fred Arnold and Susan H. Cochrane,

"Economic Motivation Versus City Lights: Testing Hypotheses About Inter-Changwat Migration in Thailand," World Bank Staff Working Paper No. 416 (Sept. 1980).

19. Kuznets, "Introduction," p. xxx. See also Section IV.1.

20. Mitchell A. Seligson, "Public Policies in Conflict: Land Reform and Family Planning in Costa Rica," *Comparative Politics,* 12 (Oct. 1979), 49–62, has pointed out the possible adverse effects of land reform in terms of fertility control objectives. See also C. Shannon Stokes and Wayne A. Schutjer, "A Cautionary Note on Public Policies in Conflict: Land Reform and Human Fertility in Rural Egypt," *Comparative Politics,* 16 (Oct. 1983), 97–104.

Bibliography

Alston, Lee J. and Schapiro, Morton Owen. "Inheritance Laws Across Colonies: Causes and Consequences," *Journal of Economic History,* 44 (June 1984), 277–287.

Anderson, James E. "A Theoretical Foundation for the Gravity Equation," *American Economic Review,* 69 (March 1979), 106–116.

Arnold, Fred and Cochrane, Susan H. "Economic Motivation Versus City Lights: Testing Hypotheses About Inter-Changwat Migration in Thailand," World Bank Working Paper No. 416 (September 1980).

Berkner, Lutz K. "Peasant Household Organization and Demographic Change in Lower Saxony (1689–1766)," in *Population Patterns,* Lee, ed., 53–69.

Berkner, Lutz K. and Mendels, Franklin F. "Inheritance Systems, Family Structure and Demographic Patterns in Western Europe, 1700–1900," in *Historical Studies,* Tilly, ed., 209–224.

Billings, John S. "The Diminishing Birth Rate in the United States," *Forum,* 15 (June 1893), 470–475.

Blodget, Samuel. *Economica: A Statistical Manual for the United States of America.* Washington, D.C., 1806.

Bogue, Allan G. *From Prairie to Corn Belt.* Chicago: The University of Chicago Press, 1963.

Carvajal, Manuel J. and Geithman, David T. "An Economic Analysis of Migration in Costa Rica," *Economic Development and Cultural Change,* 23 (October 1974), 105–122.

Coale, Ansley J. and Demeny, Paul. *Regional Model Life Tables and Stable Populations.* Princeton: Princeton University Press, 1966.

Coale, Ansley J. and Zelnik, Melvin. *New Estimates of Fertility and Population in the United States.* Princeton: Princeton University Press, 1963.

Cuca, Robert and Pierce, Catherine S. *Experiments in Family Planning.* Baltimore: Johns Hopkins University Press, 1977.

Danhof, Clarence H. *Change in Agriculture: The Northern United States, 1820–1870.* Cambridge: Harvard University Press, 1969.

Danhof, Clarence H. "Farm-Making Costs and the 'Safety-Valve': 1850–60," *Journal of Political Economy,* 49 (June 1941), 317–359.

Davis, Kingsley. "The Theory of Change and Response in Modern Demographic History," *Population Index,* 29 (October 1963), 345–366.

Demeny, Paul. "Early Fertility Decline in Austria-Hungary: A Lesson in Demographic Transition," *Daedalus,* 97 (Spring 1968), 502–522.

Dow, Thomas. "Fertility and Family Planning in Sierra Leone," *Studies in Family Planning,* 2 (May 1971), 153–165.

Dow, Thomas E. Jr. and Werner, Linda H. "Family Size and Family Planning in Kenya," *Studies in Family Planning,* 12 (June/July 1981), 272–277.

Easterlin, Richard A. "The Economics and Sociology of Fertility: A Synthesis," in *Historical Studies,* Tilly, ed., 57–134.

Easterlin, Richard A. "A Model of Rural Population Growth in the American North," a paper presented at the Landon Project Symposium, "A Blueprint for Interdisciplinary Regional History," University of Western Ontario, September 1977.

Easterlin, Richard A. "Population Change and Farm Settlement in the Northern United States," *Journal of Economic History,* 36 (March 1976), 45–75.

Easterlin, Richard A. "An Economic Framework for Fertility Analysis," *Studies in Family Planning,* 6 (March 1975), 54–63.

Easterlin, Richard A. "Farm Production and Income in Old and New Areas at Mid-Century," in *Essays,* Vedder and Klingaman, eds., 77–117.

Easterlin, Richard A., Alter, George and Condran, Gretchen A. "Farms and Farm Families in Old and New Areas: The Northern United States in 1860," in *Family and Population,* Hareven and Vinovskis, eds., 22–84.

Eldridge, H. T. and Thomas, D. S., eds. *Population Redistribution, and Economic Growth, U.S., 1870–1950* Vol. 3. Philadelphia: American Philosophical Society, 1964.

Falaris, Evangelos M. "The Determinants of Internal Migration in Peru: An Economic Analysis," *Economic Development and Cultural Change,* 27 (January 1979), 327–341.

Firebaugh, Glenn. "Population Density and Fertility in 22 Indian Villages," *Demography,* 19 (November 1982), 481–494.

Forster, Colin and Tucker, G. S. L. *Economic Opportunity and White American Fertility Ratios: 1800–1860.* New Haven: Yale University Press, 1972.

Friedlander, Dov. "Demographic Responses and Socioeconomic Structure: Population Processes in England and Wales in the Nineteenth Century," *Demography,* 20 (August 1983), 249–272.

Friedlander, Dov. "Demographic Responses and Population Change," *Demography,* 6 (November 1969), 359–381.

Fuller, W. A. and Battese, G. E. "Estimation of Linear Models with Crossed-Error Structure," *Journal of Econometrics,* 2 (May 1974), 67–78.

Gallaway, L. E., Gilbert, R. F. and Smith, P. E. "The Economics of Labor Mobility: An Empirical Analysis," *Western Economic Journal,* 5 (June 1967), 211–223.

Gallaway, Lowell E. and Vedder, Richard K. "Mobility of Native Americans," *Journal of Economic History,* 31 (September 1971), 613–649.

Glass, D. V. and Eversley, D. E. C., eds. *Population in History.* London: Edward Arnold Publishers, 1965.

Greenwood, Michael J. "The Determinants of Labor Migration in Egypt," *Journal of Regional Science,* 9 (August 1969), 283–290.

Greenwood, Michael J. "An Analysis of the Determinants of Geographic Labor Mobility in the United States," *The Review of Economics and Statistics,* 51 (May 1969), 189–194.

Grabill, Wilson H., Kiser, Clyde V. and Whelpton, P. K. *The Fertility of American Women.* New York: John Wiley and Sons, 1958.

Greven, Philip J. Jr. *Four Generations: Population, Land and Family in Colonial Andover, Massachusetts.* Ithaca: Cornell University Press, 1970.

Gutman, Robert. "The Birth Statistics of Massachusetts During the Nineteenth Century," *Population Studies,* 10 (July 1956), 69–94.

Haines, Michael R. "The Use of Model Life Tables to Estimate Mortality for the United States in the Late Nineteenth Century," *Demography,* 16 (May 1979), 289–312.

Hamilton, C. Horace. "Population Pressure and Other Factors Affecting Net Rural-Urban Migration," *Social Forces,* 30 (December 1951), 209–215.

Hareven, Tamara K. and Vinovskis, Maris A., eds. *Family and Population in Nineteenth-Century America.* Princeton: Princeton University Press, 1978.

Hicks, J. R. *The Theory of Wages.* New York: MacMillan and Company, 1932.

Higgs, Robert. "Mortality in Rural America, 1870–1920: Estimates and Conjectures," *Explorations in Economic History,* 10 (Winter 1973), 177–195.

International Conference on Family Planning in the 1980's Recommendations (Jakarta, Indonesia, April 26–30, 1981). "Family Planning in the 1980's: Challenges and Opportunities," *Studies in Family Planning,* 12 (June/July 1981), 251–256.

Isard, Walter. *Methods of Regional Analysis: An Introduction to Regional Science.* Cambridge: The M.I.T. Press, 1960.

Knodel, John E. *The Decline of Fertility in Germany.* Princeton: Princeton University Press, 1974.

Knodel, John, Havanon, Napaporn, and Pramualratana, Anthony. "A Tale of Two Generations: A Qualitative Analysis of Fertility Transition in Thailand," *Population and Development Review,* 10 (June 1984), 297–328.

Kuznets, Simon. *Economic Growth and Structure, Selected Essays.* New York: W. W. Norton and Company, 1965.

Kuznets, Simon. "Long Swings in Population Growth and Related Economic Variables," in *Economic Growth,* Kuznets, ed., 328–378.

Kuznets, Simon. "Introduction: Population Redistribution, Migration, and Economic Growth," in *Population Redistribution,* Eldridge and Thomas, eds., xxiii–xxxv.

La Sorte, Michael A. "Nineteenth Century Family Planning Practices," *The Journal of Psychohistory,* 4 (Fall 1976), 163–183.

Lee, Everett S. "A Theory of Migration," *Demography,* 3 (No. 1, 1966), 47–57.

Lee, Everett S., Miller, Ann Ratner, Brainard, Carol P. and Easterlin, Richard A. *Population Redistribution and Economic Growth, U.S., 1870–1950, Vol. 1, Methodological Considerations.* Philadelphia: American Philosophical Society, 1957.

Lee, Ronald Demos, ed. *Population Patterns in the Past.* New York: Academic Press, 1977.

Leet, Don R. "Interrelations of Population Density, Urbanization, Literacy, and Fertility," *Explorations in Economic History,* 14 (October 1977), 388–401.

LePlay, Frederic. *L'Organization de la Famille.* Paris: Tequi, 1871.

Libecap, Gary D. and Alter, George. "Agricultural Productivity, Partible Inheritance, and the Demographic Response to Rural Poverty: An Examination of the Spanish Southwest," *Explorations in Economic History,* 19 (April 1982), 184–200.

Lindert, Peter. *Fertility and Scarcity in America.* Princeton: Princeton University Press, 1978.

Lipton, Michael. "Migration from Rural Areas of Poor Countries: The Impact of Rural Productivity and Income Distribution," *World Development,* 8 (No. 1, 1980), 1–24.

Lotka, Alfred J. "The Size of American Families in the Eighteenth Century and the Significance of the Empirical Constants in the Pearl-Reed Law of Population Growth," *Journal of the American Statistical Association,* New Series 22 (June 1927), 154–170.

Malthus, Thomas Robert. *An Essay on the Principles of Population* (originally published in 1798) reprinted in *A Norton Critical Edition,* Philip Appleman, ed. New York: W. W. Norton and Company, 1976.

Matthiesson, Paul C. and McCann, James C. "The Role of Mortality in the European Fertility Transition: Aggregate-Level Relations," in *The Effects,* Preston, ed., 47–68.

Mazumdar, Dipak. *The Urban Labor Market and Income Distribution: A Study of Malaysia,* published for the World Bank. Oxford: Oxford University Press, 1981.

McInnis, R. M. "Childbearing and Land Availability: Some Evidence From Individual Household Data," in *Population Patterns,* Lee, ed., 201–227.

McInnis, R. Marvin. "Birth Rates and Land Availability in North America in the Nineteenth Century, With Special Reference to Ontario," mimeographed, Queen's University, 1972.

McNall, Neil Adams. *An Agricultural History of the Genesee Valley 1790–1860.* Philadelphia: 1952.

McNicoll, Geoffrey. "Consequences of Rapid Population Growth: An Overview and Assessment," *Population and Development Review,* 10 (June 1984), 177–240.

Meeker, Edward. "The Improving Health of the United States, 1850–1915," *Explorations in Economic History,* 9 (Summer 1972), 353–373.

Miller, Edward. "Is Out-Migration Affected by Economic Conditions?," *Southern Economic Journal,* 39 (January 1973), 396–405.

Munro, John M. "Migration in Turkey," *Economic Development and Cultural Change,* 22 (July 1974), 634–653.

Neal, Larry and Uselding, Paul. "Immigration, A Neglected Source of American Economic Growth: 1790 to 1812," *Oxford Economic Papers,* 2nd Series, 24 (March 1972), 68–88.

Parnes, Herbert S. *Research on Labor Mobility: An Appraisal of Research Findings in the United States,* Social Science Research Bulletin 65, 1954.

Pindyck, Robert S. and Rubinfeld, Daniel L. *Economic Models and Economic Forecasts.* New York: McGraw-Hill Book Company, 1976.

Potter, J. "The Growth of Population in America, 1700–1860," in *Population in History,* Glass and Eversley, eds., 631–688.

Preston, Samuel H. *The Effects of Infant and Child Mortality on Fertility.* New York: Academic Press, 1978.

Ravenstein, E. G. "The Laws of Migration," *Journal of the Royal Statistical Society,* 52 (June 1889), 241–301, also in reprint no. S-483 of the "Bobbs-Merrill Series in the Social Sciences."

Ravenstein, E. G. "The Laws of Migration," *Journal of the Royal Statistical Society,* 48 (June 1885), 167–227, also in reprint no. S-482 of the "Bobbs-Merrill Series in the Social Sciences."

Rees, P. H. "The Measurement of Migration, From Census Data and Other Sources," *Environment and Planning,* 9 (A 1977), 247–272.

Sahota, Gian S. "An Economic Analysis of Internal Migration in Brazil," *Journal of Political Economy,* 76 (March/April 1968), 218–245.

Schapiro, Morton Owen. "Land Availability and Fertility in the United States, 1760–1870," *Journal of Economic History,* 42 (September 1982), 577–600.

Schapiro, Morton Owen. "Internal Migration in the United States: Evidence From the Early 19th Century," Williams College Research Paper Series No. 47 (April 1982).

Schultz, T. Paul. "Rural-Urban Migration in Columbia," *The Review of Economics and Statistics,* 53 (May 1971), 157–163.

Schwartz, Aba. "Interpreting the Effect of Distance on Migration," *Journal of Political Economy,* 81 (September/October 1973), 1153–1169.

Seaman, Ezra C. *Essays on the Progress of Nations.* New York: C. W. Benedict, 1853.

Seligson, Mitchell A. "Public Policies in Conflict: Land Reform and Family Planning in Costa Rica," *Comparative Politics,* 12 (October 1979), 49–62.

Shah, Nasra M. "Past and Current Contraceptive Use in Pakistan," *Studies in Family Planning,* 10 (May 1979), 164–173.

Silvers, Arthur and Crosson, Pierre. *Rural Development and Urban-Bound Migration in Mexico.* Resources for the Future Research Paper R-17. Washington, D.C.: 1980.

Sjaastad, Larry A. "The Costs and Returns of Human Migration," *Journal of Political Economy,* 70 (October 1962), 80–93.

Spillman, W. J. "The Agricultural Ladder," *American Economic Review,* Supplement, 9 (March 1919), 170–179.

Steckel, Richard H. "The Economic Foundations of East-West Migration during the 19th Century," *Explorations in Economic History,* 20 (January 1983), 14–36.

Stokes, C. Shannon and Schutjer, Wayne A. "A Cautionary Note on Public Policies in Conflict: Land Reform and Human Fertility in Rural Egypt," *Comparative Politics,* 16 (October 1983), 97–104.

Taeuber, Conrad and Taeuber, Irene B. *The Changing Population of the United States.* New York: John Wiley and Sons, 1958.

Thompson, Warren S. and Whelpton, P. K. *Population Trends in the United States.* New York: McGraw-Hill Book Company, 1933.

Tilly, Charles, ed. *Historical Studies of Changing Fertility.* Princeton: Princeton University Press, 1978.

Tilly, Charles. "The Historical Study of Vital Processes," in *Historical Studies,* Tilly, ed., 3–59.

Tilly, Charles. "Questions and Conclusions," in *Historical Studies,* Tilly, ed., 335–350.

Todaro, Michael P. "A Model of Labor Migration and Urban Unemployment in Less Developed Countries," *American Economic Review,* 59 (March 1969), 138–148.

Tucker, George. *Progress of the United States in Population and Wealth in Fifty Years.* New York: Press of Hunt's Merchant's Magazine, 1855.

Turner, Frederick Jackson. *The Frontier in American History.* New York: Henry Holt and Company, 1921.

Turner, Frederick Jackson. "The Significance of the Frontier in American History," a paper read at the meeting of the American Historical Association in Chicago, July 12, 1893, reprinted in Turner, *The Frontier,* 1–38.

U.S. Bureau of the Census. *U.S. Census of Population: 1960, Vol. I, Characteristics of the Population, Part 1, United States Summary.* Washington, D.C.: U.S. Government Printing Office, 1964.

U.S. Bureau of the Census. *Historical Statistics of the United States, Colonial Times to 1957.* Washington, D.C.: U.S. Government Printing Office, 1960.

U.S. Bureau of the Census. *Seventh Census of the United States: 1850.* Washington, D.C.: Robert Armstrong, Public Printer, 1853.

van de Walle, Etienne. "Alone in Europe: The French Fertility Decline Until 1850," in *Historical Studies,* Tilly, ed., 257–288.

Vedder, Richard K. and Klingaman, David C., eds. *Essays in Nineteenth Century Economic History: The Old Northwest.* Athens, Ohio: Ohio University Press, 1975.

Vinovskis, Maris A. *Fertility in Massachusetts from the Revolution to the Civil War.* New York: Academic Press, 1981.

Vinovskis, Maris A. "A Multivariate Regression Analysis of Fertility Differentials Among Massachusetts Townships and Regions in 1860," in *Historical Studies,* Tilly, ed., 225–256.

Vinovskis, Maris A. "Socioeconomic Determinants of Interstate Fertility Differentials in the United States in 1850 and 1860," *Journal of Interdisciplinary History,* 3 (Winter 1976), 375–398.

Walker, Francis A. "Immigration and Degradation," *The Forum,* 11 (August 1891), 634–644.

Warwick, Donald P. *Bitter Pills.* Cambridge: Cambridge University Press, 1982.

Willcox, Walter F. "The Change in the Proportion of Children in the United States and in the Birth Rate in France During the Nineteenth Century,"

Publications of the American Statistical Association, 12 (March 1911), 491–495.

World Bank. *World Development Report 1984.* Published for the World Bank. Oxford: Oxford University Press, 1984.

Wrigley, E. A. "Fertility Strategy for the Individual and the Group," in *Historical Studies,* Tilly, ed., 135–154.

Yasuba, Yasukichi. *Birth Rates of the White Population in the United States, 1800–1860.* Baltimore, Johns Hopkins University Press, 1962.

Index